THE SOUP BOOK

Brigid Allen was born and brought up in the West Country. She studied History at Oxford and has worked as an archivist, manuscript cataloguer and scholarly editor in London and New York. Her interest in soup-making began during a frugal period in London when she lived near the Inverness Street vegetable market and the ethnic food shops of Camden Town. In 1982 she moved with her husband and son to Oxford, initially to spend a summer doing research for a history of English diaries. She now divides her time between writing about food, cultivating vegetables and working on historical and literary topics.

The
SOUP BOOK

BRIGID ALLEN

PAPERMAC

For David and Edmund

First published 1993 by
PAPERMAC
a division of Pan Macmillan Publishers Limited
Cavaye Place London SW10 9PG
and Basingstoke

Associated companies throughout the world

ISBN 0 333 58224 1

1 3 5 7 9 8 6 4 2

A CIP catalogue record for this book is available from
the British Library

Typeset by Florencetype Limited, Kewstoke, Avon
Printed by Mackays of Chatham PLC, Chatham, Kent

Soup forms the first course of the meal of those who dine in the true sense of the term, but its importance as a part of the every day diet is not sufficiently appreciated by the multitude.

Mrs Beeton, Household Management

Tonight she contented herself with the automatic ceremony of giving him what she remembered, more or less correctly, when planning the menu, as being his favourite food – *zelyonïya shchi*, a velvety green sorrel-and-spinach soup containing slippery hard-boiled eggs and served with finger-burning, irresistibly soft, meat-filled or carrot-filled or cabbage-filled *pirozhki* – peer-rush-KEY, thus pronounced, thus celebrated here, for ever and ever.

Vladimir Nabokov, Ada

I am in the kitchen participating in John Millet's prodigious soup making. He makes a soup with Jane Goldman's excess tomatoes, donning her butcher's apron and pushing up his sky blue wrist bands to reveal the bronze sinews of his lovely wrists. He requires, for his creation, the addition of ground rice, egg yolks, a great deal of grinding in a stone mortar and some careful sieving. Jonathan and I are delegated to dip strips of bread first into a pool of melted butter and then into Parmesan cheese which Jane draws out of her larder in a large caterer's pack. These are then toasted in the oven and are to be eaten with the soup . . . We eat at the kitchen table when the children have finished, and all agree that the soup is quite delicious.

Barbara Trapido, Brother of the More Famous Jack

ACKNOWLEDGEMENTS

For their help towards the publication of this book, I should especially like to thank Alan Davidson; my agent, Caroline Davidson; Emily Green of *The Independent* Features Section; and my editor at Macmillan London, Judith Hannam. Long-standing friends to whom I am particularly grateful for their enthusiasm and support include Sally Baldwin, Pamela Taylor and John and Dorothee Wallis.

I acknowledge the kind permission of Faber & Faber Limited to quote from *What the Light Was Like* (1986) by Amy Clampitt.

CONTENTS

A Note About Measurements and Ingredients

The recipes are intended to feed four people. As a rough rule of thumb, every 275 ml/½ pint of water or stock specified serves a single consumer.

Although vegetables do not come in uniform sizes, I have written the recipes on the assumption that all onions, carrots, potatoes, etc., are of medium size. Where the recipe calls for something different it is specified.

As a general rule, I use old potatoes when making soup, rather than new, although it is usually perfectly acceptable to use either. Occasionally a recipe does call for a particular kind, and in these instances I have specified the type required.

INTRODUCTION

During the past twenty years, cooking in the West has experienced a revolution and soup, like many other things, has changed. Novelty and freshness are in; old, stale tastes out. Every restaurant with a remotely innovative cook seems to produce its own original soups, often blending local produce with exotic flavours such as ginger, lemon grass or other oriental spices. A new tradition of soups has evolved, combining flavours that would once have seemed unorthodox together but are now thoroughly familiar. Celery or leek with Stilton, chickpea and tomato, and carrot with coriander and orange are all to be found both in tins in supermarkets and on the counters of delicatessen shops and sandwich-bars. In the home, the electric liquidizer and food processor have made experimentation easy; while the year-round availability of fresh herbs and many exotic or tender vegetables has freed the routine of soup-making from the limitations of the seasons.

Because soup is relatively easy and flexible to make, it has been very much in the forefront of gastronomic innovation. Even before the new eclecticism in cooking, soup was recognized as a light and healthy, potentially vitamin-rich kind of food, and was readily transported from one culture to another. The international classics – minestrone, borshch, gazpacho, vichyssoise – have been current throughout the western world for the best part of this century, following after the *haute cuisine*-inspired fashion for delicately garnished *consommés*. My own first memories of eating abroad are coloured by the tastes and appearance of soups: a wonderfully subtle, strong vegetable soup (perhaps celery flavoured with chervil or lovage) in a Paris convent the summer that I was sixteen; a fiery, nourishing chilli bean soup in a Kansas City diner; *tortellini con brodo* in Florence; and proper minestrone, black with spinach leaves and rich with tomato-suffused flecks of olive oil.

The recurrent appeal of soup may go back to its historic origins as one of the simplest, most basic forms of cooked food. The bread and red lentil soup ('broth' or 'pottage'; 'relish' or 'sauce' in another version of the Bible) which Jacob sold to Esau in return for his elder brother's birthright remains one of the most comforting and satisfying of foods for someone as physically worn out as Esau had become from his work in the fields. Bread and soup, with the bread as the staple nourishment and the soup as a condiment to moisten it and make it more appetizing, have recurred, with variations as in north-western India where the bread is dipped into small bowlfuls of semi-liquid curry, throughout western and Middle Eastern civilizations. Often, in an Esau-like frame of mind, I have wandered through London at cold winter lunchtimes, longing for good bread (virtually an impossibility unless made at home and carried round with one), and good soup to dip it in, rather than the highly salted, monosodium glutamate-spiked offerings of slot-machines, pubs and canteens.

Most cooking is opportunistic; and anyone who has partially lived off the land, making soup in a country cottage out of young spring nettles or sorrel gathered from the fields, can share something of the feeling of medieval cooks who made a broth of 'wortes' in Lent. *Honey From a Weed* (1986), Patience Gray's account of cooking in primitive conditions in various parts of southern Europe, vividly describes what it is like to grub up bitter herbs from a hillside to make into spring salad or soup. Throughout southern Europe, where meat was scarce and limited to an occasional goat or lamb, soup and supper were more or less synonymous for centuries of peasant life, with soup very often only a relish to moisten the bread. The bourgeois soup course at the evening dinner, followed inexorably by meat or fish, probably evolved from the earlier peasant custom as much out of ancestral piety or habit as out of an appreciation of the healthiness of soup or of the simpler pleasures of life.

In Britain, meanwhile, where vegetables have always taken second place to meat, the story was somewhat different, as in other parts of northern and central Europe. Meat cooked over a spit was a luxury for lavishly provided households; and the more usual method of cooking it, by slow seething in a pot, resulted in large amounts of sometimes fatty, sometimes flavoursome and concentrated broth. In medieval England there were a number of soups or soup-like dishes, many of them for non-meat days, such as pease soup or porridge, which varied in consistency from liquid to solid; mussels stewed in their own juices; leeks cooked in oil and wine. Broth itself was a food for poorer people, invalids and children, unless garnished with dumplings or meat tartlets to make it into an appetizing dish. Between the sixteenth and nineteenth centuries the meat- and pastry-loving English seem to have been generally prejudiced against soups of any kind in favour of more solid food; and broth, or skilly as it was sometimes known, became associated with the workhouse, school or orphanage, where a watered-down version of pease porridge was a standard filler, and where the quantities of anaemic broth produced by boiling beef or mutton might be served instead of ale for breakfast, alternately with gruel. Charles Lamb, describing the Christ's Hospital food of his schooldays in the 1780s, remembered both 'pease soup . . . coarse and choking' and 'boiled beef . . . with detestable marigolds floating in the pail to poison the broth'.

In private houses, cooks could make both pease soup and broth more palatable than they were in institutions; yet their status remained low, pease soup doing duty as a homely dish for winter, and broth being largely kept for those who could not eat or afford to have meat. Apart from pea soup made with fresh garden peas in summer, vegetable soup of any kind seems to have been almost non-existent. In the 1790s Parson James Woodforde referred several times in his diary to eating pea soup, usually in winter or spring. At a fairly elaborate dinner with neighbours he encountered veal soup as part of a first course; and at home he once dined simply on 'Giblet-Soup & a rost Rabbit'. Other writers of the second half of the eighteenth century who chronicled their main meals seem never to have tasted soup from one year's end to the next.

The Victorians and their immediate predecessors, by contrast, loved soup, or at least respected it as a solitary survival from the first courses of many dishes eaten by their richer ancestors. Turtle soup, a symbol of luxury from Regency to Edwardian times, appeared not only at grand dinners but in masculine strongholds such as Birch's eating-house in Cornhill in the City of London. White soup, a more feminine luxury, was served at balls in Jane Austen's day, and became degraded only later from a confection of ground almonds, chicken stock and cream into an economical, character-less slop made with turnips and milk. An early nineteenth-century fashion for French food among the rich brought foreign cooks to work in England, with their knowledge of *consommés* and *potages*; and the new, French-influenced fashion of serving separate courses in succession, rather than laying out several courses on the table together, became the archetype of the late Victorian middle-class eating-pattern of soup, fish, entrée, sweet.

Vegetable soup, then, apart from pea soup, has had a relatively short-lived existence of less than two centuries in Britain; and, even within that period, it has moved capriciously in and out of fashion. In Eliza Acton's *Modern Cookery for Private Families* (1845), there are carrot, Jerusalem artichoke, chestnut and apple ginger soups; a vegetable mulligatawny made with cucumbers, apples and vegetable marrow; and a pea soup, surely French-influenced, using fresh green peas with cucumbers, parsley, mint and lettuce hearts. It is not for these soups, however, that we remember the Victorians so much as for their rich, meaty game soups and *consommés*; their mock turtle and meat-based mulligatawny soups; their thin gravy soups, calf's foot broth and invalid beef tea. When charitable soup kitchens came into being in the cities towards the middle of the nineteenth century, the soup that they dispensed was nearly always meat soup, sometimes made from unpopular 'preserved Australian meat' which the working classes, given the choice, preferred not to touch.

Thick or clear; white or brown; garnished or ungarnished; vegetable or meat: by the early years of this century soup was as susceptible to classification as it was unsusceptible to inventiveness on the part of the average cook. Chefs were drilled in several dozen different ways of presenting *consommé*; while, further down the social scale, the housewife learned to thicken broth with pearl barley, tapioca, sago or rice. Nutritionally unimportant to most people who consumed it, soup had become a badge of respectability, dividing those who dined in style from the Mr Pooters and their inferiors who only ate high tea.

When servants all but finally disappeared at the outbreak of the Second World War, domestic soup-making went with them. The thin white pepperpot and thick brown gluepot soups, so expressive of a national reverence for anything connected with meat, lingered on mainly in provincial hotels, hospital wards and the dining-halls of institutions. When tinned soup came to the housewife's rescue after the war, many of the traditional flavours (or attempts at them) such as oxtail and mulligatawny were there. Tinned soup, however, established itself as a classless, lunchtime convenience food rather than an instant first course for a formal dinner; and the most popular flavour turned out to be tomato, denatured, bland, and as unlike anything home-made as it could be.

How much have things changed since then? In a series of Gallup Polls conducted between 1947 and 1973, tomato soup kept its favoured place as the first course in the respondents' choice of a perfect meal, regardless of expense. More recently its popularity has wavered, judging by attempts to revamp it by adding ethnic touches such as chickpeas or beans, or

'Mediterranean' ones such as garlic powder and dried herbs. Yet the proportion of British households buying tinned soup, according to a recent survey, is still more than three times higher than the average for ten other European countries, ranging from the Republic of Ireland to Greece.★

To devotees of tinned or packeted soups, who enjoy their strong saltiness, uniformity of thickening and the stimulus which they give the less discerning palate with copious doses of monosodium glutamate, home-made soup may never represent anything but a time-consuming chore. It can take a while to wean oneself from predictable tastes and textures and to develop an appreciation of the subtle and unexpected. Once begun, however, soup-making can develop into a gastronomic and nutritional adventure. Which soups make the best use of seasonal produce, such as asparagus or chestnuts; which need meat stock, and which are better made without it; which are suitable for a dinner-party, a family supper in winter, a journey with a thermos, or a summer lunch in the garden with one or two friends? Which are nourishing enough to make a meal in themselves, and which are not? All these questions eventually find their own answers; but experimentation with combinations of ingredients can continue almost indefinitely, to make the habit of soup-making interesting for a lifetime.

At this point protests may arise from believers in the virtues of sticking to well-tried, classic recipes such as one finds in many collections of soups from around the world. Elizabeth David, in her section on soups in *French Provincial Cooking* (1960), probably the most influential of all books on food to appear in England since Mrs Beeton's *Household Management*, warns against the dangers of finding soup too appetizing and thus spoiling the many other courses which are to follow. She also warns against the hapless 'creative' cook who cannot resist substituting her own ideas for traditional recipes. When making soup, in particular, she must be kept on as tight a leash as possible, 'a saucepan of innocent-looking soup being a natural magnet to the inventive, and to those who pride themselves on their gifts for inspired improvisation'.

★ Great Britain, 75%; West Germany 48%, Holland 42%, Belgium 41%, Ireland 33%, France 14%, Denmark 13%, Italy 8%, Spain 4%, Portugal 3%, Greece 1%; *Daily Telegraph*, 12 February 1991.

Before the inventive bridle and reach for their liquidizers, it may be best to look at these remarks in the context of their time. 'Using up', a national British pastime in the days of large joints of meat and no refrigerators, was the enemy of freshness and true originality. Rissoles, bubble-and-squeak, cottage pie all derived from an economy in which one ate one really fresh dish at the beginning of the week, on Sunday, and lived on leftovers for much of the rest of the time. Elizabeth David herself recounts how a contemporary of her youth advised her to 'take pretty well everything in the larder . . . add some water, and in due course . . . some soup would emerge'. With the advent of the liquidizer, at about the same time as the waste-disposal unit and the appearance of *French Provincial Cooking*, dedicated users-up could simply blend together any of the remnants of Sunday's roast potatoes, vegetables and gravy and call them soup. No wonder, then, that perfectionists reacted against this slap-happy approach and insisted that soup was not soup in the true sense of the word unless it could be recognized as a traditional classic.

During the last thirty years, however, our national eating-habits have changed enormously. In supermarkets, back-to-back with the aisles of tinned and new-look, bottled soup, are displays of organic vegetables; growing herbs in pots; exotic fresh peas and beans flown in from tropical regions in January. Garlic, ginger and chillies can be found in almost every small neighbourhood greengrocery shop. Our inspiration in cooking no longer comes from the traditions of continental Europe but from the East, and from a kind of melting-pot approach to the ingredients and techniques of both East and West. As so often happens in cultural matters we in Britain lag far behind the United States, where food has a cleanness and eclecticism which have barely begun to be felt here. Similarly, in terms of healthy eating, we are not yet generally as well-educated in taste and awareness as much of America, where the Californian health-food movement of the 1960s set a pattern to be followed later by the young and progressive throughout the western world.

For those who want to eat healthily, home-made soup is one of the best possible options, especially if treated as a main course for lunch and for

supper one evening every week or so. For vegetarians its benefits are obvious, since it is one of the most concentrated ways of eating a variety of
vitamin- and calcium-rich root and leaf vegetables, as well as pulses, beans,
yoghurt, chestnuts, shellfish, olive oil, garlic, spices, mushrooms or avocado
pears. Contrary to the precepts laid down in conventional cookery books
of a generation or two ago, soup does not need to be made using either
meat stock or a thickening of butter and flour, eggs or cream. Some soups
need meat stock to unify the flavours of different vegetables, especially in
chunky, mixed soups such as minestrone, or to give a strong background to
dried beans, split peas or vegetables of indeterminate character. Most,
however, can rely on the taste of the right combination of vegetables,
accentuated by slow sweating in oil before any water is added, and by sea
salt, black pepper, garlic, herbs or proper Japanese soy sauce (*tamari* or
shoyu). As for thickening, this is usually unnecessary if the ingredients
are liquidized rather than pushed through a sieve or *moulin-légumes*. With
certain vegetables such as very stringy celery or old broad beans with very
tough skins, or with fish that contains fine bones, it may be better to use a
moulin-légumes; but in general the fibre that this excludes forms a natural
thickening in liquidized soups and does less harm than good.

When making soup, then, think in terms of nourishment rather than of
creating an elegant first course, and you may find that you have created the
basis of a main meal which needs no more than good bread and perhaps
cold meat, cheese or a pudding to be complete. Tinned or packeted soup
is not usually satisfying enough to make a proper meal even at lunchtime,
since it is full of sugar, salt and added thickenings and flavourings. Home-
made soup contains all the vitality of fresh ingredients in a much higher
degree of concentration than in the bought kind, and can also be enriched
with other ingredients which would never find their way into tinned
soup, such as extra virgin olive oil. A plain, bland oil such as sunflower oil
(recommended by most nutritionists as a polyunsaturated oil, giving positive protection against the build-up of fatty deposits in the arteries) is often
best for the preliminary cooking of the vegetables in very delicately
flavoured soups or in others such as curried soups in which the main taste

might clash with that of olive oil. Olive oil, on the other hand, a mono-unsaturate with neither positively protective nor harmful qualities, brings out the best in bland vegetables such as celery, leeks and potatoes, and strengthens the character of tomato-based soups which are flavoured with garlic and herbs. Olive oil and good bread are natural companions; and I like to float an extra tablespoonful or two of olive oil on the surface of chunky, mixed vegetable soups, or add it to others with a rough, unusual taste such as potato, olive and anchovy or roast garlic and potato.

Making soup regularly can change your life by introducing new, subtle flavours and combinations of vegetables and other ingredients into it. It is a perfect vehicle for herbs such as parsley, lovage, thyme, marjoram and basil, and has a range of textures from the roughest (unpuréed vegetables, split peas, brown lentils) to the smoothest (potato, summer spinach, sorrel). One of my favourite ingredients in a puréed soup is roast garlic, which has a melting texture and a sweetness of taste quite unlike the notorious roughness of the raw, squeezed clove. Curried soups are improved by Greek yoghurt, a good source of nourishment with a lively but not too sharp taste. Mushrooms will combine well with leafy vegetables such as watercress and summer spinach, especially when pre-cooked in oil and garlic and enlivened at the end of cooking with a tablespoonful of good soy sauce. Potatoes are an invaluable thickening in soups made of watery vegetables such as celery, and combine well with peppers, olive oil, tomatoes, leeks and cabbage. Like the editor of Janet Ross's late Victorian classic, *Leaves from Our Tuscan Kitchen*, I find potato generally 'a better thickening for soup than flour, partly because it is a vegetable itself and not a cereal and also because the consistency is fresher and more palatable'.

Can one live on soup? Probably not; yet I have met many people, predominately middle-aged and self-employed or based mainly at home, who have told me how much they love home-made soup and how much they rely on it for sustenance, especially at winter lunchtimes. Again, there are advantages in having home-made soup on hand in the refrigerator or freezer for those evenings when you need a quick, hot, soothing meal and cannot face an omelette, a thawed pizza, a mound of spaghetti or a tin of baked beans. Such has been the force of the green revolution, even among non-vegetarians, that a meal with no vegetable content now seems even less acceptable than one with no obvious protein content would have seemed twenty or thirty years ago. Some soups, such as fish, leek or French onion, age quite rapidly and should be eaten within two or three days of being made if they are not to become rancid in the refrigerator. One friend of mine, however, insists that most soups mature with age and are best if kept standing for up to a week.

In compiling this book I have assumed the use of an electric liquidizer which makes extra thickening of soup largely unnecessary. Those with larger goblets, holding up to 1.5 litres/2 ½ pints, are better than the smaller kind unless you are making really tiny quantities of soup. Many of these plastic goblets may crack if filled with boiling or nearly boiling liquid; so allow the soup to cool for 10–15 minutes between simmering and liquidizing. Make sure, too, that the top fastens on firmly and unambiguously, since few things are more painful than thick, hot soup on one's face, hands, clothes and kitchen ceiling. If determined, you can make soup in almost any kind of saucepan; but the best thing to have is a large, heavy, cast-iron casserole with a well-fitting lid, in which you can first sweat the vegetables in oil, then simmer them in water or stock. As most soup involves cutting up several different kinds of vegetable, you will also need a large, plain, workmanlike board or clean surface, an efficient peeler and a sharp knife.

Some of the distinctions which I have made in the arrangement of this book may seem to be little more than arbitrary. This is especially true of those between summer and winter vegetable soups and between soups which need or do not need to be made with meat stock. As far as summer and winter soups are concerned, our constant influx of imported vegetables from around the world means that only home-grown ones can be said to have any true season. Many imported vegetables, on the other hand, have less taste than the home-grown kind, a defect which is particularly noticeable in soup. While summer spinach, for example, tastes much the same wherever it is grown (and therefore counts as a winter vegetable

in this book, being more readily available in winter as an imported vegetable than in summer as a home-grown one), other vegetables, such as
American asparagus, Egyptian broad beans and Guatemalan, Zimbabwean
or Zambian mangetout peas are too forced and standardized when grown
for export to be interesting in soup. On the whole, therefore, I have
assumed that soups will be made with home-grown vegetables in season
unless, like spinach, these are in unreliable supply. For the use of stock, I
have set aside a number of soups which do not work well without this.
Other soups, especially those in the winter vegetable category, such as
celeriac, celery, Jerusalem artichoke or leek and potato, are often improved
by the use of chicken stock but do not actually need it. If you hate the idea
of making chicken-bones into stock, are vegetarian or have other reasons
for avoiding a meaty or poultry flavour, ignore the former group and make
the latter using water. If the vegetables are good, their overall quality will
be little different either way.

Finally, bread. Without good bread, soup does not begin to make a
whole meal. The Spanish practice of including bread in soup (as in the
original gazpacho) underlines this principle; for in poorer countries bread
was the meal, and any liquid, whether vegetable- or meat-flavoured,
merely served to help it down. Like soup, good bread is now being reinvented, in compensation for the years in which bread meant a dreary kind
of white flannel which existed only as a vehicle for sweet or fatty spreads. I
therefore include a short section on home-made bread at the end of this
book. Like the recipes for soup which precede it, the bread recipes in this
section are very much my own and are not exhaustive. Rather than rep-
resenting any particular school of cookery or tradition, they should be seen
simply as new (or new-ish) departures which may inspire other cooks to
do something entirely different.

Oxford
February 1993

SUMMER VEGETABLE SOUPS

NOT USING STOCK

Basic Asparagus Soup

Like strawberries in June and July, fat bundles of asparagus in May and June are the classic, irresistible sign of an English summer. Buy lots; it is never around for very long, except in its out-of-season, imported form, when it can be ignored. Go for the plumper stalks with compact tips like unopened hyacinth flowers, and do not buy any whose tips smell musty and rotten, as they sometimes do.

The advantage of making asparagus into soup is that it quickly transforms this perishable vegetable into a state in which it keeps quite well (3–4 days), and in which it will not be ruined by a few minutes' overcooking as it can be when boiled. This soup is a variation on the conventional cream of asparagus, omitting the cream.

---

900 g/2 lb asparagus
6 spring onions
40 g/1½ oz butter
850 ml/1½ pints water

sea salt
25 g/1 oz flour
150 ml/¼ pint milk

Cut the asparagus into 2.5 cm/1 in lengths, throw away the bottom 2.5 cm/1 in of each stalk and any further pieces of stalk which seem completely hard and white, and separate the tips from the remaining lengths of stalk. Wash the tips and stalks, scrubbing away any rotten parts. Wash and chop the spring onions into 1 cm/½ in lengths, discarding the green parts. In a heavy, covered pan, soften the spring onions and the asparagus stalks in 15 g/½ oz of the butter over a gentle heat for 5–10 minutes. Cover them with the water, bring this to the boil, add a pinch of sea salt and simmer for 15–20 minutes. Drain the asparagus and spring onions, reserving the liquid in which they cooked.

Meanwhile, in another pan, make a *roux* by melting the remaining butter, stirring in the flour and gradually adding the milk until you have a thick sauce. Gradually stir in the asparagus water until this, too, has thickened; add the spring onions and asparagus stalks and the uncooked tips; simmer together for a minute or two, then liquidize. If you prefer, leave out a few tips to add whole after liquidizing, return the soup to the pan and reheat gently until the tips are just cooked through.

ASPARAGUS AND MUSHROOM SOUP

Many of my soups include mushrooms as an incidental ingredient, since mushrooms, accented by *shoyu* or *tamari* (the properly aged, Japanese-style soy sauce, available in health-food shops), give a savoury taste and smooth texture to soups made from the softer, more delicate-tasting vegetables such as asparagus, watercress, spinach and courgettes.

12 thick asparagus spears	*2 large cloves garlic, peeled and sliced*
15 g / ½ oz butter, plus 1 tablespoon	*275 ml / ½ pint milk*
olive oil	*425 ml / ¾ pint water*
3 large spring onions, washed and	*½ teaspoon sea salt*
chopped	*freshly ground black pepper*
450 g / 1 lb cultivated mushrooms,	*freshly grated nutmeg*
washed and halved	*1 teaspoon shoyu or tamari*

Cut up and wash the asparagus as in the preceding recipe. Reserve the tips and chop the stalks into 2.5 cm/1 in long pieces. Melt the butter in a heavy pan with 1 tablespoon of olive oil to prevent it from browning. Add the asparagus stalks, the spring onions, the mushrooms and the garlic, and soften over a gentle heat for 10–15 minutes with the lid on the pan. When the mushrooms have given off a good amount of juice, remove a few of them, chop finely and put them on one side to keep warm. Add the milk and water to the contents of the pan, bring it to the boil and simmer for 15 minutes. Season with half a teaspoon of sea salt, freshly ground black pepper and freshly grated nutmeg and allow to cool a little before liquidizing.

Return the soup to the pan, add the uncooked asparagus tips and the reserved, finely chopped-up mushrooms, heat gently until the tips are just cooked through, then add 1 teaspoon of *shoyu* or *tamari* to bring out the deep mushroom flavour.

Broad Bean Soup with Tomatoes and Garlic

I have been growing broad beans for about twelve years, and have been addicted to them from the beginning. Even where I started, in a front-garden plot in one of the more polluted parts of inner North London, where neighbours warned me solemnly of the lead which I should be consuming if I ate my own produce, I found the smartness of their black and white flowers uplifting on dull, grey days in June. Now I make soup from the tops of the plants (*see* Green Velvet Soup, p. 115), which, if removed early, help to keep down blackfly. Later on, once the first grey-green, tender beans have been eaten, any tougher survivors can be made into a soup in which their nutty taste combines well with plenty of garlic. The new season's garlic, with its soft outer layer and thick, juicy stalk, works particularly well in a soup such as this.

2 onions, peeled and chopped

3 tablespoons olive oil

12 large cloves garlic

sea salt

4 large tomatoes, skinned and chopped

2–3 teaspoons fresh thyme or marjoram

freshly ground black pepper

pinch of sugar (optional)

900 g/2 lb (shelled weight) broad
    beans, shelled

1.2 litres/2 pints water

6 large fresh basil leaves

Soften the onions in 3 tablespoons of olive oil in a heavy, covered pan. After 5–10 minutes peel and halve 3–4 of the garlic cloves and stir them in, allowing them to soften without browning. Crush the rest of the garlic in a mortar with a little sea salt and add it to the contents of the pan with the tomatoes and the thyme or marjoram leaves. Season with salt, pepper and a little sugar if the tomatoes lack sweetness and cook uncovered for 5–10 minutes, raising the heat a little and breaking up the tomatoes with a wooden spoon. Add the beans, cover with 1.2 litres/2 pints of water, bring to the boil and simmer for 20–30 minutes. Allow to cool slightly, then liquidize and sprinkle with the fresh, torn-up basil leaves before serving.

A nice, robust soup, good with bread and cheese and a warm, southern French red wine.

Broad Bean Soup with Pesto

A good soup for imparting flavour to the middle-aged broad beans of high summer. Beware, however, of trying to make it with the leather-skinned, mealy specimens which have next to no taste left in them; the result will be unrewarding.

Pesto and broad beans are one of those combinations of tastes which seem immediately classic and right. With pasta, pesto can be overpoweringly strong, either because it contains too much freshly crushed raw garlic or because the garlic has turned rancid (which is only too likely to happen if the pesto is bottled for sale). In soup the taste is tamed and diffused without losing the immediate, rich fragrance of crushed basil leaves. Two southern European soups from neighbouring areas, the *soupe au pistou* of Nice (which was part of Italy until 1860) and the *minestrone Genovese* of Genoa, both contain beans and pesto against a background of other vegetables. Olive oil, garlic, pine nuts, beans and cheese were all items which regularly appeared in the Ancient Roman diet, if not necessarily together. Cheese and pine nuts, however, appear in combination in Apicius's well-known cookery manual of (possibly) the first century AD, as do beans with olive oil and aromatic herbs; and it needs only a small leap of the imagination or change in custom for all these ingredients to merge together, as they do in this soup.

2 onions, peeled and chopped	*PESTO*
2 carrots, peeled and chopped	2 cloves of garlic, peeled
2 tablespoons olive oil	sea salt
675–900 g / 1½–2 lb (shelled weight) broad beans, or 2.3–2.7 kg / 5–6 lb beans in the pod	12–15 large fresh basil leaves
	40 g / 1½ oz pine nuts or broken cashew nuts (optional)
1.5 litres / 2½ pints water	40 g / 1½ oz grated Parmesan
1 teaspoon sea salt	3–4 tablespoons extra virgin olive oil

Soften the onions and carrots in 2 tablespoons of olive oil in a heavy, covered pan. After 10–15 minutes, add the shelled beans and cook for a minute or two longer with the lid on. Cover with the water, add 1 teaspoon of sea salt, bring to the boil and simmer for 20 minutes while making the pesto.

For this you will need quite a large mortar or a small pudding basin wedged in such a way that it will not skid. Crush the garlic with a pinch of sea salt, add the basil leaves and pound them into the garlic until you have an aromatic, green sludge. If you are using nuts, grind them into this mixture with the pestle until they have merged with the basil and garlic. Stir in the grated cheese, then liquefy the mixture by gradually adding 3–4 tablespoons of olive oil until the pesto is loose but not runny. Add the pesto to the soup either before or after liquidizing, depending on the texture you prefer.

A filling start to an informal supper. In high summer this could be followed by a simple salad of Little Gem lettuces, basil and rocket with an olive oil and garlic dressing, and by cold ham or a creamy cheese such as Vignotte or Brie with the rest of a loaf of freshly baked, home-made bread.

NOTE

Must I use fresh pesto? you may ask. I once tried a jar of shop-bought pesto, containing 'basil, vegetable oil, Parmesan cheese, pecorino cheese, pine kernels, cashew nuts, salt, acidity regulator, glucono delta-lactone, garlic, marjoram'. Not even when it was first opened did this pesto contain more than an allusion to the tastes of fresh basil, fresh Parmesan cheese and non-rancid garlic. The least essential part of a fresh pesto is probably the nuts, which give a binding effect to the mixture when it is eaten as a sauce but are not really necessary when it dissolves into soup. No nuts at all, or bland, relatively tasteless cashew-nut pieces, are better than the stale and expensive pine nuts which sometimes sit around for months too long on the shelves of delicatessen and health-food shops.

BEETROOT AND FRUIT SOUP

The inspiration for this soup was an early autumn visit to a friend, who when we left presented us with a beetroot from her husband's allotment and a basket of windfall pears from the neighbouring garden. Unpeeled beetroot is a dull-looking vegetable; and, although it smells nice when newly cooked, it has depressing associations for many of us with school Monday lunches and soggy, cold rounds of sweetish beetroot well soaked in vinegar before leaking their red juices over lumpy, grey mashed potato. When newly washed and peeled, however, a beetroot has a brilliant, lively, almost translucent appearance. Forgetting vinegar, I looked for ways of bringing out its essential sweetness by combining like with like: in this case, seasonal fruit and the mild, English onions which also come into season early in the autumn. This soup gains in flavour as it cools, and improves with reheating (a common characteristic of other soups containing apple), making it a good offering for someone whose arrival may be late or delayed.

1½ large, mild English onions, peeled and chopped
2 tablespoons sunflower oil
1 very large or 2 medium-sized uncooked beetroot

2 Cox's Orange Pippin or similar eating apples
2 large, juicy dessert pears
1.2 litres/2 pints water
1 generous teaspoon sea salt

Soften the onions in 2 tablespoons of sunflower oil in a heavy, covered pan. Peel and wash the beetroot under running water, which will transform a dull, purplish object into a blood-red, juicy globe. Cut it into dice and stir it into the onion. Continue softening for 10–15 minutes more. Peel, core and slice the apples and pears, stir them into the onion and beetroot, cover with the water and season with sea salt. Bring to the boil and simmer for 30 minutes, then liquidize. The beetroot should still have a fairly firm texture so that it stands out with a slight roughness among the other ingredients.

Cold Carrot Soup with Ginger

'There was some carrot soup yesterday – so good it almost broke my heart,' wrote Emily Eden, the society letter-writer and future author of *The Semi-Detached House* and *The Semi-Attached Couple*, lamenting the departure of their cook in 1826 from the house which she shared with her brother, Lord Auckland, in Lower Grosvenor Street.* Food, consumed though it was in enormous and luxurious quantities by the upper classes of the Edens' day, does not often make such a specific appearance in their letters. If it does, it is usually banquet food rather than the light and wholesome food of every day. Only very rarely does a letter reveal a glimpse of large, cool larders; of the walled enclosures of country-house kitchen gardens, from which hampers of produce made their way weekly to London during the spring and summer season; and of the acres of onions and broccoli, cabbages and artichokes grown in the London nursery gardens from Kensington and Battersea westward along the riverbanks to Barnes, Isleworth and Brentford.

Carrot soup, one of the great nineteenth-century culinary delights of the ordinary kitchen, is now almost unknown outside the coriander-and-orange belt, since it depended on delicacy and freshness and could not therefore be successfully translated into tinned form. To the French, and those who had French-trained cooks, it was *potage Crécy*, for which the juiciest garden carrots were stewed in butter, then simmered in stock, sieved and garnished with parsley, chervil and lovage. To the English, with their taste for oriental spices, it was often something livelier, like the 'Buchanan Carrot Soup' which Eliza Acton included in her *Modern Cookery for Private Families* (1845) and which consisted of stock, Patna rice and a spoonful of fine curry powder or paste.

*Emily Eden to Maria Copley, n.d. (16 February 1826), Grey of Howick Papers, Durham University Library.

Emily Eden, although familiar with Indian spices from her youth, had always been inclined to suspect and ridicule anything which seemed dangerously exotic. When she and her brother sailed for India in 1836 on his appointment as Governor-General, they took with them every possible protective European comfort including their own French chef. We may assume, therefore, that the carrot soup made by their cook ten years earlier had been bland, buttery or creamy and perhaps herby, but uncurried.

This gingery soup is one to make with stubby, ordinary shop carrots which need waking up, and may be regarded as a fiery alternative to plain, healthful carrot juice. It helps if you have an electric juicer which can convert a handful of carrots into a glassful of bright, nutty-tasting juice. Bought carrot juice will, however, do as a substitute for home-made.

---

2 onions, peeled and chopped
2 tablespoons sunflower oil
900 g / 2 lb carrots, peeled and chopped
  (or, if you have no juicer, 450g /
  1 lb carrots and 250–300 ml /
  8–10 fl oz bought carrot juice)

4 cloves garlic, peeled and chopped
15 g / ½ oz ginger root, peeled
sea salt
1 litre / just under 2 pints water
1 sprig of mint

Soften the onions in 2 tablespoons of sunflower oil in a heavy, covered pan. Peel the carrots, cut half of them into dice (or all of them, if you do not intend to make your own juice) and add these to the onions to soften for 10–15 minutes. Carrots which have not been softened tend to resist liquidizing and come out as obdurate lumps. Crush the garlic and ginger in a mortar with a little sea salt and stir them in. Cook gently for a minute or two, then cover with the water, season with a teaspoon of sea salt, bring to the boil and simmer for 20–30 minutes, adding a sprig of mint before the end of cooking. Allow to cool slightly, remove the mint and liquidize. Add the remaining, juiced carrots or the bought carrot juice to the soup, swirling the bright orange juice into the paler, spicy-tasting purée. Serve cold.

CARROT AND APPLE SOUP WITH MARJORAM

This is a pleasant lunchtime soup to serve with bread and cheese or cold ham.

2 large, mild English onions, peeled and chopped	*8 medium to large carrots, peeled and chopped*
2 tablespoons sunflower oil	*just over 1.2 litres/2 pints water*
15 g/½ oz butter	*1 teaspoon sea salt*
4 Cox's Orange Pippin or similar eating apples, unpeeled, cored and chopped	*freshly ground black pepper*
	1 tablespoon fresh marjoram leaves

Soften the onions in 2 tablespoons of sunflower oil in a heavy, covered pan. Add the butter and the carrots and continue softening for 10–15 minutes, making sure that the onions do not brown; then add the apples. Soften for another 5–10 minutes, stirring occasionally, until the apples have begun to disintegrate, then cover with the water, bring to the boil and simmer for 20–30 minutes. Allow to cool slightly, then liquidize, adding the sea salt, a good grinding of black pepper and the marjoram before you do so.

CARROT SOUP WITH PARSLEY OR LOVAGE

Other herbs which go well with carrots are parsley, mint and lovage. If using parsley or lovage, omit the apples and substitute an equal quantity, or rather less, of potatoes. Apple mint would go well in this soup.

Mayorquina with Chinese Greens

A soup for gardeners. By Chinese greens I do not mean Chinese cabbage, that tasteless, watery vegetable of a thousand supermarket counters. A few years ago the seedsmen Thompson & Morgan Ltd, of London Road, Ipswich, Suffolk, introduced a new strain of prolific, spinach-like greens from China named Tendergreen, and another with rougher, almost borage-like leaves named Big Top. These hardy, late summer vegetables will grow in almost any soil and are claimed to have a high vitamin content. When cooked like spinach, I found them dull and slightly bitter; but they go extremely well in soup when left unpuréed, giving it an exciting, green taste without the slippery texture of sorrel or summer spinach. Here they replace the traditional leeks and cabbage in *Mayorquina*, a borrowing from Elizabeth David's *French Country Cooking*, 1966.

2 onions, peeled and chopped

3 red peppers, de-seeded and chopped

5 tablespoons extra virgin olive oil

3–4 potatoes, scrubbed and diced

8 large cloves garlic

4 tomatoes

sea salt

freshly ground black pepper

pinch of sugar (optional)

350 g / 12 oz Chinese greens,
    preferably Tendergreen, cleaned

just over 1.2 litres / 2 pints water

Soften the onions and the peppers in 3 tablespoons of the olive oil in a heavy, covered pan. After 10–15 minutes add the scrubbed and diced unpeeled potatoes and 6 of the garlic cloves, peeled and cut in half. (This soup does not go through the liquidizer, so take care to chop everything slightly smaller than usual.) Skin and roughly chop the tomatoes and crush the remaining two garlic cloves in a mortar with a little sea salt. Add the tomatoes and garlic to the contents of the pan. Season with salt, pepper and a little sugar if the tomatoes are very acid. Cook uncovered, breaking up the tomatoes, over a higher heat for 5–10 minutes as if for a sauce, then add the Chinese greens and the water, bring to the boil and simmer for 20–30 minutes. Before serving, stir in another 1–2 tablespoons of extra virgin olive oil and pour the soup over slices of home-made bread in soup plates.

COURGETTE SOUP

Despite the large amount of garlic in this soup, the distinctive taste and lovely smoothness of courgettes prevails. They can, in fact, taste finer in a soup of this kind than when plainly fried or baked as a vegetable, or smothered in a strong tomato sauce.

2 onions, peeled and chopped	8 large cloves garlic
3–4 carrots, peeled and chopped	sea salt
3 tablespoons olive oil	4 tomatoes, peeled and chopped
8 small or 4 large courgettes	1.2 litres/2 pints water
4 smallish potatoes, unpeeled	6 black peppercorns

Soften the peeled and chopped onions and carrots in 3 tablespoons of olive oil in a heavy, covered pan for 5–10 minutes. Rinse, dry and cut the courgettes into 1 cm/½ in slices, and wash and dice the potatoes. Add the courgettes and potatoes with all but 1 of the whole, peeled garlic cloves to the pan. Stir them gently together with the carrots and onions and continue softening with the lid on the pan for another 10–15 minutes, stirring every now and then to make sure that the courgettes do not brown. Crush the remaining clove of garlic in a mortar with a little sea salt and add to the pan with the tomatoes. Cook a little faster, stirring frequently, for

5–10 minutes as if for a sauce, until the tomatoes have disintegrated, then add the water, 1 teaspoon of sea salt and half a dozen black peppercorns. Bring to the boil and simmer for 20–30 minutes before liquidizing. The soup will be delicately coloured and flecked with the dark green of the courgette skins.

COURGETTE AND RICE SOUP

A filling, piquant alternative to the previous soup. Eaten with good bread and plenty of freshly grated Parmesan, this makes a complete light meal in itself.

Odd though the combination of chilli with courgettes may seem, it is in fact extremely good, and can be used with imported Spanish courgettes as a warming, winter evening soup.

50 g/2 oz brown rice
sea salt
2 onions, plus 1 small onion, peeled
  and chopped
2 tablespoons sunflower oil
½ a bell-shaped chilli pepper, de-seeded
8 large cloves garlic, peeled and sliced
pinch of sugar

4 tomatoes, or half a 400 g/14 oz tin
  chopped tomatoes
4 carrots, peeled and chopped
3 tablespoons olive oil
4 large courgettes, sliced
just over 1.2 litres/2 pints water
freshly ground black pepper
grated Parmesan

Cook the rice in twice its volume of water with a pinch of sea salt at a gently simmering temperature for 30 minutes, or until the water has been absorbed. Some kinds of brown rice take up to 10 minutes longer than others to cook, depending on their type and the extent to which they have been processed. The more rice you use, the less water, proportionately, is needed.

Soften the small onion in 2 tablespoons of sunflower oil in a heavy, covered pan. After 5 minutes add the finely chopped chilli pepper and a sliced clove of garlic and continue softening for another 5–10 minutes. Add the tomatoes, a pinch of sea salt and a small pinch of sugar and cook uncovered for another 10 minutes over a slightly raised heat until the tomatoes have disintegrated. Stir the cooked rice into the sauce until it is completely coated. (This may be done some time in advance.)

To make the soup, soften the 2 remaining onions and the carrots in 3 tablespoons of olive oil in a heavy, covered pan. After 10–15 minutes add the courgettes and the remaining garlic, sliced. Stir these round well, cover the pan again and continue softening for a further 10 minutes, then cover with the water seasoned with 1 teaspoon of sea salt and some freshly ground black pepper, bring to the boil and simmer for 20–30 minutes. Liquidize, then stir in the tomato-and-rice mixture, return to the heat until warmed through and serve thickly sprinkled with Parmesan.

COURGETTE, MUSHROOM AND SPINACH SOUP

A savoury, dark green soup, uncommonly good at lunchtime or as the basis of a simple, family supper. Like many of these summer vegetable soups, it is equally practicable to make in winter, with imported spinach and courgettes. For lunch, try it with home-made Oat Bread (see recipe p. 174) thickly spread with blue Brie; for supper, with garlicky meatballs and new potatoes or brown rice.

1 onion, peeled and chopped

2 carrots, peeled and chopped

3 tablespoons olive oil

3 large courgettes, sliced

6 cloves garlic, peeled and sliced

225 g/8 oz mushrooms

225 g/8 oz summer spinach

1 teaspoon sea salt

freshly ground black pepper

1.2 litres/2 pints water

1 tablespoon shoyu or tamari

Soften the onion and carrots in 2 tablespoons of olive oil in a heavy, covered pan. After 5–10 minutes, add the courgettes and 4 of the sliced garlic cloves. Continue cooking gently with the lid on, stirring occasionally, for another 10–15 minutes.

Meanwhile rinse and cut up the mushrooms and stew them gently with the remaining garlic in another tablespoon of olive oil in a covered frying-pan for 10–15 minutes until soft. Wash the spinach thoroughly and discard any thick or broken stalks and any wilted or slimy leaves. Add the spinach to the courgettes, carrot and onion; season with 1 teaspoon of sea salt and some freshly ground black pepper; cover with the water, bring to the boil, add the mushrooms and garlic and simmer for 15–20 minutes. Cool a little, liquidize and add the *shoyu* or *tamari,* to bring out a savoury taste.

LEEK AND POTATO SOUP (SUMMER VERSION)

When possible, I like to serve soup with other dishes rather than simply as a preliminary to something heavier and more solid. This has sometimes caused difficulty with conventionally brought-up guests, especially those who have been through the routines of a British boarding-school and whose idea of a proper meal is firmly structured into three courses. Yet a vitamin-rich vegetable soup can perfectly well complement a simple meat dish such as lamb chops (which I recommend especially as an accompaniment to this garlic, tomato and herb flavoured leek and potato soup), without an extra vegetable dish being necessary. In the eighteenth century, soup took its place in the first course of large, formal meals among a number of other different dishes, all of which were to be tasted and enjoyed without any one of them being allowed to predominate.

2 onions, peeled and chopped

2 carrots, peeled and chopped

3 tablespoons olive oil

900 g/2 lb leeks

900 g/2 lb potatoes, unpeeled

7–8 tomatoes, skinned and chopped

sea salt

7–8 cloves of garlic, peeled and crushed

1 tablespoon fresh thyme or marjoram

freshly ground black pepper

pinch of sugar (optional)

just over 1.2 litres/2 pints water

Soften the onions and carrots in 3 tablespoons of olive oil in a heavy, covered pan. Wash the leeks, discarding the base and the coarsest green parts of each, and slit them lengthways on opposite sides of the stem to release trapped pockets of dirt. Chop them into 2.5 cm/1 in lengths, stir them into the onions and carrots and continue softening for a further 10–15 minutes, stirring occasionally. Then add the scrubbed and diced potatoes, the tomatoes, the crushed garlic, pounded up in a mortar with a little sea salt, and the leaves of thyme or marjoram. Cook as if for a sauce, seasoning with salt, pepper and sugar if necessary, for another 5–10 minutes until the tomatoes begin to disintegrate. Cover with the water, bring to the boil, simmer for 20–30 minutes, then liquidize.

Good with Parmesan croûtons for a light lunch (see overleaf).

Parmesan Croûtons

MAKES ENOUGH FOR 2 PORTIONS

4 slices home-made wholemeal/granary
   or other bread

40 g/1½ oz freshly grated Parmesan
3 tablespoons extra virgin olive oil

Heat a cast-iron or other thick frying-pan over a moderately high heat while you cut the bread and (if you are quick about it) grate the cheese. Pour in the oil and make sure that it is hot but not smoking. Quickly fry the bread on one side until it is crisp but not too dark brown, then turn the slices over in the pan and cover them generously with Parmesan. To finish, pat the cheese down firmly, then reverse the slices again and let the cheese just melt through contact with the hot metal of the pan. Remove with a spatula, cut each slice into small cubes and serve as a side dish rather than in the soup.

Parmesan Croûtons with Garlic

Garlic-lovers can follow the above recipe, spreading a small crushed clove of garlic on each slice of bread before sprinkling with the cheese.

Plain Croûtons

The above recipe omitting the Parmesan.

Mushroom and Coriander Soup

This soup provides a use for those bunches of fresh coriander which often seem to be wilting as they lie on greengrocers' stalls or outside oriental food shops. My edition of Mrs Beeton describes the smell of coriander as 'unpleasant', suggesting a memsahib-like revulsion from exotic, 'native' foods. To me the smell is haunting, rather like that of willow-herb in late July and August, and the taste an elaboration on the smell. In this soup, which has certain affinities with the French *Potage aux Champignons à la Bressane* (see Elizabeth David, *French Provincial Cooking*, 1970), coriander replaces the traditional parsley as an accompanying herb.

450 g / 1 lb cultivated or field
   mushrooms
2 tablespoons olive oil
2 cloves garlic, peeled
sea salt

1–2 bunches fresh coriander
110–175 g / 4–6 oz fresh wholemeal
   or granary bread
850 ml / 1½ pints milk
freshly ground black pepper

Throw the mushrooms into a basinful of cold water, pick them out at once and wipe them clean and dry with kitchen paper. Chop them as small as you can with a sharp knife. Heat 2 tablespoons of olive oil in a heavy pan, tip the mushrooms into it, add the garlic crushed with a little sea salt and cook slowly, covered, for 10–15 minutes until the mushrooms have produced quite a lot of their own juice. Wash the coriander, discard most of the stalks and any yellow or spoilt leaves, and chop the remaining leaves finely on a board. Crumble the bread and chop the crumbs into the heap of coriander leaves until they have absorbed its green juices. Add most of the milk to the mushrooms and bring it to simmering point, allowing it to cook gently for 5–10 minutes before adding the breadcrumb-and-coriander mixture. Continue simmering for a further 5–10 minutes, adding more milk if the mixture seems too thick and seasoning with salt and pepper. Leave the soup to cool slightly before serving. Do not liquidize, since part of the charm of this soup is the contrast between the finely chopped, solid ingredients and the delicately flavoured liquid.

MUSHROOM, ONION AND WATERCRESS SOUP

A lovely soup, which justifies the use of three separate pans for its preparation. Served at a summer outdoor lunch, it calls for little else except good bread, creamy cheese, a salad and perhaps an open fruit tart.

450 g/1 lb onions	50 g/2 oz wholemeal or brown flour
1.2 litres/2 pints water	275 ml/½ pint milk
450 g/1 lb mushrooms, cleaned and roughly chopped	sea salt
	freshly ground black pepper
5–6 cloves garlic, peeled and crushed	freshly grated nutmeg
2 tablespoons olive oil	3 bunches watercress, washed and
50 g/2 oz butter	chopped

Peel and quarter the onions, cover them with the water seasoned with a pinch of sea salt and boil them gently, covered, for about 15 minutes. Drain, reserving the onion liquid. Meanwhile stew the mushrooms gently with the garlic in 2 tablespoons of olive oil until they have given off their liquid. In another, larger pan, melt the butter and stir in the flour. Brown or wholemeal flour gives a more interesting taste to this soup than white; and the malted grains in granary flour are not out of place. Gradually stir in the milk, then the onion water, until the soup has the consistency of a very thin sauce. Season this with sea salt, freshly ground black pepper and nutmeg; add the cooked onions, the mushrooms in their liquid and the watercress; simmer together just below bubbling point for a few minutes, then cool slightly and liquidize.

ONION AND WATERCRESS SOUP

Omitting the mushrooms and garlic, the above soup can be made in a simpler form as a bland, reviving onion and watercress soup, very good (for example) as a light meal after a long journey.

NETTLE BROTH

In the 1950s a lower corner of our terraced, late-Victorian garden was rankly overgrown with nettles. Firmly rooted in ancient compost heaps, they must have taken hold there during the war, when the greenhouse caved in, the suburban tennis lawn became a tussocky wilderness which my father used to scythe, and the box and laurel hedges overgrew into child-sized caves and tunnels. Once or twice, impelled by thrift and perhaps by a memory of wartime Ministry of Food leaflets on vitamins and healthy eating, my mother went down with gardening gloves and a basket to snip off nettles. These appeared, boiled into a dark green, stringy mass, as a vegetable. 'Just like spinach . . . ' she explained. Whatever the nourishing properties of nettles, they did not catch on; and I do not remember her making them into this strong, aromatic broth, as I found myself doing on a frugal holiday in a Devon farm cottage years later.

Nettles are full of Vitamins A and C, and are good for gout and rheumatism as their alkalinity helps to dissolve uric acid crystals. The time to pick them is ideally April or May, when they have developed enough stalk to grasp firmly but before they become dark green, large-leaved, coarse and woody. Use thick gloves and concentrate on the tips well above the dark red part of the lower stalk.

1 carrier-bag freshly picked spring or
  early summer nettles
1 onion, peeled and chopped
1 carrot, peeled and chopped

1 tablespoon sunflower oil
1.2 litres/2 pints water
1 teaspoon sea salt
½–1 tablespoon shoyu or tamari

In the sink, separate the brighter, fresher leaves and stalks of the nettles from the rest with scissors before rinsing those which you intend to use in a colander. Soften the onion and carrot in the oil in a heavy, covered pan before adding the nettles and covering with the water and 1 teaspoon of sea salt. Bring to the boil, simmer for 20–30 minutes, then strain off the liquid, season it with *shoyu* or *tamari* if it seems to need strength and drink it as a plain, cleansing broth. It has a tonic and stimulating taste.

NETTLE BROTH WITH VEGETABLES

Alternatively, for a thin soup with vegetables in it, make the nettle broth without the onion and carrot; cook them separately, adding diced celery and any other vegetables you like and strain the broth over them, simmering for an extra 10–15 minutes.

Green Pea Soup with Meat Juice

Pea soup, with its pejorative connotations of thick, yellow fog or heavy bacon stock, had become debased by the late nineteenth century from Parson Woodforde's 'good Peas Soup' of a century earlier, which must have been the light, brilliantly green confection beloved of the early Victorians. No nonsense then about using floury, old peas for soup; for, as Eliza Acton pointed out, while it might be wasteful to make soup out of new peas, they should not be so far gone that 'their fine sweet flavour is entirely lost, and the dried ones would have almost as good an effect'. Pea soup, indeed, is one of the few classic English soups to have been wholly vegetable-based without recourse to a background of meat stock. (Bacon stock belongs essentially with dried peas to make a filling, unsubtle dish.) Victorian cooks liked to flavour or bulk out fresh pea soup with herbs and salad vegetables, while avoiding anything which might detract from its greenness. Eliza Acton recommended both lettuces and cucumbers; Mrs Beeton, lettuces, leeks and mint; and Queen Victoria's former chef Francatelli (*The Cook's Guide*, 1861), spring onions, parsley and mint. Francatelli also issued a special warning against using sorrel, a much more popular herb in Victorian times than it is now, for fear of making the soup 'both yellow and sour'.

Now that many shop-bought peas are already past the halfway stage indicated by Eliza Acton, we cannot be too fussy about colour (as, presumably, the poor could not when reduced to using the mealy, dried peas which gave rise to the idea of the 'pea-souper'). Garlic, peppers and tomatoes are good modern accompaniments to bring out the taste of indifferent peas without extinguishing it altogether. Another good addition is jellied meat juice or 'glaze', recommended by Francatelli to enrich what could otherwise have been a rather insipidly delicate soup, but also excellent for enhancing more powerful combinations of flavours. This lovely juice, when produced by conventional English roasting methods, is usually incorporated in gravy and eaten directly with the roast meat. In Italy, as *sugo di carne*, it quite often appears separately from the meat as a sauce to pour over pasta, and may be confused with the thicker meat sauce which also goes under that name. A sure way of producing enough for a soup or pasta is by pot-roasting, a method which particularly suits a neat, round half-leg of lamb, as shown overleaf.

1 large carrot, peeled and chopped	250 ml/8 fl oz juice from roast lamb
8–10 large cloves garlic, peeled	350g/12 oz shelled weight or
2 tablespoons olive oil	1 kg/2¼ lb unshelled fresh peas
3 tomatoes, skinned and chopped	1.2 litres/2 pints water
sea salt	a handful of sorrel leaves, washed
freshly ground black pepper	120 ml/4 fl oz pesto sauce (see
sugar (optional)	page 19) (optional)

Soften the carrot and all but 1 of the garlic cloves in 2 tablespoons of olive oil in a heavy, covered pan. After 10 minutes add the tomatoes and the remaining garlic clove, crushed with a little sea salt, and cook uncovered as if for a sauce, breaking up the tomatoes with a wooden spatula. Season with salt, pepper and a little sugar if necessary. After 5–10 minutes, stir in the meat juice and the raw, shelled peas. Cover with the water, bring to the boil and simmer for 20 minutes, adding the torn-up sorrel leaves 5 minutes before the end. Liquidize and, if you want a richer taste still, serve with pesto sauce handed separately.

Pot-Roasted Half Leg of Lamb

half leg lamb (fillet end), roughly   *olive oil*
   900 g/2 lb in weight   *8–10 large cloves garlic*
1 sprig rosemary

Place the lamb in a covered casserole on the rosemary sprig after trimming off all the fat and rubbing the joint all over with olive oil. Cook with the lid on in a moderately hot oven, 190°C, 375°F, gas mark 5, for 1–1½ hours, adding peeled, whole garlic cloves to roast in the juices after about 30–45 minutes. The abundant juice from the joint can be sopped up into a dish of lightly mashed cauliflower florets and roast garlic, or used for braising celery or in pea soup, as p. 37.

Green Pea Soup with Peppers

A slightly oriental-tasting soup, in which the sharp sweetness of peppers brings out the flavour of peas which might otherwise be past their best.

2 onions, peeled and chopped   *1 small knob ginger root, peeled and*
2 carrots, peeled and chopped   *chopped*
2 tablespoons olive oil   *sea salt*
2 green or yellow peppers, or one of   *350 g/12 oz (shelled weight) fresh*
   each, de-seeded and chopped   *peas*
3–4 cloves garlic, peeled   *1.2 litres/2 pints water*
                               1–2 tablespoons shoyu or tamari

Soften the onions and carrots in 2 tablespoons of olive oil in a heavy, covered pan. After about 10 minutes stir in the de-seeded, chopped peppers, and when these have softened a little, after another 5–10 minutes, add the peeled and chopped ginger root and garlic, crushed in a mortar with a little sea salt. A small knob of ginger, the size of a large pea or a very small marble, is all that this soup needs, since the taste of ginger should be refreshing rather than overpowering. When the peppers have softened add the peas, cover with the water, season with a teaspoon of sea salt, bring to the boil and simmer for 20 minutes before liquidizing. Add *shoyu* or *tamari* to taste before serving.

Green Pea Soup with Potato and Peppers

A simpler pea-and-pepper soup can be made by omitting the ginger, garlic and *shoyu* or *tamari* but adding a washed, diced, unpeeled potato with the peas. Include a little extra salt, and serve with chopped mint and freshly ground black pepper after liquidizing.

Mangetout Pea Soup

Despite their tender, tropical image, fostered by imports of limp, new, air-freighted peas from Zambia and Guatemala, mangetout peas are extremely easy to grow in cold soils in the more waterlogged parts of southern England. I have been growing them for several years on a railway bank on clay, and have found them sweeter, more characterful, and of course much cheaper than the year-round, imported kind. Their chief defects are an eccentric knobbliness and a tendency to grow on unnoticed on the plants until they are as large, if not as tough, as ordinary pea pods. Both of these can be remedied by turning them into soup instead of trying to serve them plainly boiled, stir-fried or steamed. This simple soup contains the highly concentrated, sweet taste of pea pods, which economical cooks used to achieve when cooking ordinary peas by stripping out the tough outer layers and adding the tender inner layers of the pods to cook with them.

1 large onion, peeled and chopped	*1 teaspoon sea salt*
1 large carrot, peeled and chopped	*1 litre/just under 2 pints water*
2 tablespoons olive oil	*shoyu or tamari, to taste*
700 g/1½ lb mangetout peas	*fresh peas, for garnish*

Soften the onion and carrot in 2 tablespoons of olive oil in a heavy, covered pan. Top-and-tail and de-string the mangetout peas and cut each of them into 2 or 3 pieces. After 10–15 minutes, when the onion and carrot have softened, stir in the mangetouts, add the sea salt and the water, bring to the boil and simmer for 15–20 minutes. Liquidize, season with *shoyu* or *tamari* and add a garnish of a few raw, new peas.

A rich, greenish-orange soup with a delicate savoury taste.

TOMATO, GARLIC AND BREAD SOUP

The English outdoor tomato harvest is a tricky thing. However early you sow the seeds or put out the young plants, the speed with which the fruit will ripen is unpredictable. Sometimes you can come home from holiday in August to find a jungle of plants weighed down with trusses of red fruit; while at other times they are still obstinately green in October or even

November. A mild autumn can prolong the outdoor ripening season until, at some point in the middle of October, you will probably uproot the plants and take a wheelbarrow-load of greenish tomatoes to finish ripening indoors in drawers and cupboards. Once the chutney-making urge has subsided, and long after those disciplined ranks of Italian plum tomatoes have been sun-dried, made into *ragù* or bottled, you will need to devise soups and sauces to use up the late-ripening surplus. Even if these tomatoes have a slightly sunless, vinegary taste, they can still be made into soup with plenty of garlic, herbs and a thickening of good, home-made bread, which reduces the sharpness to a minimum.

4 sticks celery, washed	*sea salt*
1–2 tablespoons olive oil	*pinch of sugar*
8 large cloves garlic, peeled	*1 litre / just under 2 pints water*
700 g / 1½ lb tomatoes	*4 slices good wholemeal or granary*
1 tablespoon thyme or marjoram	*bread*
freshly ground black pepper	*fresh basil, if available*

Soften the de-stringed and chopped celery sticks in 1–2 tablespoons of olive oil in a heavy, covered pan. Add the halved garlic cloves; and, when these have softened for 5–10 minutes, add the roughly chopped tomatoes. Bigger ones will need skinning by immersion in near-boiling water, but cherry tomatoes can keep their skins since these will not be perceptible after liquidizing. Crumble in a tablespoon of thyme or marjoram leaves, add pepper, sea salt and a little sugar, and cook uncovered for 5–10 minutes, breaking up the tomatoes. Cover with the water, bring to the boil and simmer for 15–20 minutes, then add the torn-up bread and liquidize. Sprinkle with fresh basil before serving.

Garlic, bread, tomatoes and olive oil have natural affinities with one another, whether in soup or in a simple, pleasantly untidy salad.

Tomato, Garlic and Potato Soup with Herbs

2 onions, peeled and chopped
1 tablespoon olive oil
12 large cloves garlic, peeled and halved
2 red-skinned potatoes, washed and
   diced
8 tomatoes, skinned and chopped
1 teaspoon sea salt

freshly ground black pepper
pinch of sugar (optional)
1 tablespoon fresh thyme and
   marjoram
1 litre/just under 2 pints water
1 tablespoon fresh parsley
1 tablespoon fresh basil, if available

Soften the onions for 10–15 minutes in olive oil in a heavy, covered pan. Add the garlic cloves and the potatoes. Stir together for a minute in the oil, then add the tomatoes, sea salt, black pepper and a little sugar if necessary and cook together uncovered, breaking up the tomatoes, as if for a sauce. Crumble in 1 tablespoon of thyme and marjoram leaves. After about 10 minutes' gentle stirring, cover with the water, bring to the boil and simmer for 15–20 minutes before liquidizing. Finely chop the parsley, discarding all stalks, and sprinkle 1 tablespoon of the leaves over the surface of the soup with an equal quantity of torn-up basil leaves.

WINTER VEGETABLE SOUPS

NOT USING STOCK

JERUSALEM ARTICHOKE SOUP

The Jerusalem artichoke, *Helianthus tuberosus*, was first imported into Europe from Massachusetts at the beginning of the seventeenth century. Perhaps because it is despised as a native food, it is hard to find in the vegetable markets of Boston now and is probably more popular, especially as a soup-vegetable, in England. After growing Jerusalem artichokes on my allotment, where the sunflower-like plants formed a solid windbreak seven or eight feet high, I began to understand how people can feel overwhelmed by them and how their use may have died out in polite American society. Yet they make a very good soup and combine surprisingly well with other vegetables such as tomatoes and red peppers.

The Victorians, who could be highly sensitive to nuances of flavour, loved a bland, stock-based soup made from these slightly earthy-tasting tubers, and enjoyed the biblical pun which gave rise to the widespread name 'Palestine Soup'. (As many books have explained, 'Jerusalem' was in fact a corruption of the Italian word *girasole*, meaning sunflower, because of the resemblance between the plants.) In *Modern Cookery for Private Families*, Eliza Acton recommended a quite un-biblically lavish version of the soup, calling for 1.35 kg/3 lb of artichokes, 2.5 litres/4½ pints of veal stock and 570 ml/1 pint of 'rich boiling cream'. A leaner alternative could be made using mutton broth, more artichokes, and milk instead of cream; and this was probably the version available to undergraduates at Corpus Christi College, Oxford, in the 1870s, to be brought up to their rooms at any time of day from the buttery, with the alternatives of gravy, pea, carrot, ox-cheek, mock turtle and Julienne soups. Christ Church, on the other hand, a grander college frequented by young aristocrats and future cabinet ministers, provided no vegetable soup in the 1880s. Gravy soup, with or without a poached egg in it, mulligatawny and mock turtle (as no doubt served to the mathematics don Charles Lutwidge Dodgson) were the standard daytime restoratives, with a further choice between clear and thick oxtail and hare soup.

When buying artichokes look for firm, unwrinkled ones, since these are easier to peel than the kind which have become tired and floppy. Some writers recommend conserving flavour by cooking the washed artichokes in their skins, then peeling them while hot before serving. In soup, however, this creates an organizational problem similar to that of removing fishbones in the process of making fish soup. I prefer the lazy way, and peel the artichokes first in order to be able to forget about them. If you particularly like the flavour of the skins, one answer is to grow artichokes yourself and lift some in September when the tubers are marble-sized like early new potatoes. These need only a gentle scrub before cooking, and have a wonderful flavour either eaten whole or as the main ingredient of a soup.

2 onions, peeled and chopped　　　　　*just over 1.2 litres/2 pints water*
2 carrots, peeled and chopped　　　　　*1 teaspoon sea salt*
2 tablespoons olive oil　　　　　　　　*6 black or green peppercorns*
700 g/1½ lb Jerusalem artichokes

For this simplest of artichoke soups, soften the onions and carrots for 10 minutes in 2 tablespoons of olive oil in a heavy, covered pan. Peel and wash the artichokes, cutting each one into several pieces, and add them to the onions and carrots, stirring them in well. Continue softening for 5–10 minutes, then add the water, sea salt and half a dozen black or green peppercorns. Bring to the boil, simmer for 30 minutes and liquidize. Artichokes need a surprising amount of cooking and underdone ones can ruin a soup, so it is better to overdo rather than to economize on the cooking time.

ARTICHOKE AND RED PEPPER SOUP

The combination of peppers, potatoes and garlic is usually a good one; and in this soup it is complemented by the earthy taste of the artichokes.

2 onions, peeled and chopped

3 large red peppers, de-seeded and
   chopped

3 tablespoons olive oil

900 g/2 lb Jerusalem artichokes

2 potatoes, unpeeled

5–6 cloves garlic, peeled

1.5 litres/2½ pints water

2 teaspoons sea salt

Soften the onions and the peppers in 3 tablespoons of olive oil in a heavy, covered pan. Meanwhile wash and peel the artichokes, halve or quarter any large ones, scrub the potatoes and cut them into dice. When the onions and peppers have softened for 10–15 minutes, add the crushed garlic, then the artichokes and potatoes. Stir together well and continue softening, covered, for another 5–10 minutes. Add the water and sea salt, bring to the boil and simmer for half an hour before liquidizing.

NOTE

If you are cooking informally, this soup could be served simultaneously with a light main dish. One of my favourites is a baked dish of noodles and potato *gnocchi*, layered with tomato sauce, roast garlic and lightly fried courgettes, served with finger-lengths of steak stirred into it and with a generous topping of Parmesan cheese.

ARTICHOKE AND TOMATO SOUP

A different taste altogether.

2 smallish onions, peeled and chopped
2 tablespoons olive oil
700 g / 1½ lb Jerusalem artichokes
5–6 tomatoes, skinned and chopped,
    or 1 400 g / 14 oz tin of tomatoes
3–4 cloves garlic, peeled

1 tablespoon fresh thyme and / or
    marjoram
sea salt
freshly ground black pepper
pinch of sugar (optional)
1.2 litres / 2 pints water

Soften the onions in 2 tablespoons of olive oil in a heavy, covered pan. After 10 minutes add the peeled, washed and diced artichokes, the skinned and roughly chopped tomatoes or the tinned tomatoes, 1 tablespoon of chopped thyme and/or marjoram leaves and the garlic, crushed in a mortar with a little sea salt. Raise the heat a little and cook uncovered as if for a sauce, breaking up the tomatoes. Season with 1 teaspoon of sea salt, freshly ground black pepper and a little sugar if the tomatoes are fresh and very insipid. After 5–10 minutes cover with the water, bring to the boil, simmer for 30 minutes and liquidize.

ARTICHOKE, LEEK AND MUSHROOM SOUP

A rich, densely flavoured soup in which the taste of artichokes does not dominate, but provides a pleasant background to the mushrooms and the leeks. It has certain affinities with other soups containing mushrooms, notably Asparagus and Mushroom and Mushroom, Onion and Watercress, both included in the section on summer soups.

450 g / 1 lb Jerusalem artichokes	*110 g / 4 oz mushrooms, cleaned and*
3 tablespoons olive oil	*roughly chopped*
2 carrots, peeled and chopped	*1.2 litres / 2 pints water*
1 large or 2 small leeks, washed and	*1 teaspoon sea salt*
chopped	*6 black peppercorns*
3 cloves garlic, peeled and chopped	*1 tablespoon shoyu or tamari*

Peel and wash the artichokes, cut up each one into several pieces and put them to soften in 2 tablespoons of olive oil in a heavy, covered pan. Add the carrots and the leeks and cook together gently for another 10–15 minutes. Meanwhile, stew the mushrooms with the garlic in another tablespoon of olive oil in a covered frying-pan until they have given off a copious amount of liquid. Cover the artichokes, leeks and carrots with the water, add 1 teaspoon of sea salt and half a dozen black peppercorns, bring to the boil and simmer for 20–30 minutes. Towards the end of this time, add the mushrooms with their liquid and the *shoyu* or *tamari* for a clean, savoury taste. Cool a little and liquidize.

CABBAGE AND POTATO SOUP

The potatoes, not the cabbage, should dominate this earthy-tasting soup; so make sure that they are floury and characterful (King Edwards or Desirée are good), and that the cabbage has not lain around the kitchen for long enough to acquire a bitter taste. Caraway, which flavours this soup, was a favourite herb in medieval and later English cooking, and still persists as a flavouring of bread and many other dishes in central Europe. In England it became, like ginger, predominantly a sweet spice, and fell out of favour altogether with the demise of such Victorian delicacies as caraway comfits and seed cake. With its unexpected, fresh taste pervading the food when the seeds are bitten into, caraway is the perfect spice to enliven dull cabbage and to marry together two mild, earthy flavours, as in this soup. When grown as an annual or perennial herb it will flourish in most English gardens, and makes an attractive, tall border plant with white, lacy flowers succeeded by the distinctively stripy seeds. You can, of course, buy packeted caraway seeds in supermarkets rather than drying your own; but then half the fun and probably part of the freshness of cooking with them is lost.

1 large or 2 smallish onions, peeled and chopped	350 g/12 oz firm white cabbage, finely chopped
2 tablespoons olive oil	1 teaspoon caraway seeds
6–8 garlic cloves, peeled	1 teaspoon sea salt
4 potatoes, unpeeled	1.2 litres/2 pints water

Soften the onion in 2 tablespoons of olive oil in a heavy, covered pan. Add the halved garlic cloves and the cabbage and cook all together, stirring occasionally, for 10 minutes. Cabbage burns easily, so keep the heat low and pay special attention to the edges of the pan where it is most inclined to stick. When the cabbage has softened, add the scrubbed and diced, unpeeled potatoes, the caraway seeds, sea salt and water. Bring to the boil, simmer for 20–30 minutes, then liquidize.

NOTE
Given the English fondness for potatoes and cabbage as vegetable accompaniments to roast meat, it is perhaps surprising that we have never evolved a national cabbage-and-potato soup. One reason may have been the resistance of cabbage to ordinary sieving; another, the cultural separate-

ness of the cabbage and the potato, which on English plates have nearly always sat primly apart, complementing one another but never blending. In Continental cookery, cabbage and potatoes occur together in a number of 'big', meat-based soups from the Catalan thick soup and eastern French *potée* to the Russian *shchi*. They can also be combined smoothly in a sauerkraut-and-potato 'Farmer's Soup', used in Holland as a vehicle for sausage and bacon (see *Encyclopedia of European Cooking*, ed. Musia Soper, 1962), but recurring further east wherever meat happens to be in short supply. I have eaten a lovely version of Farmer's Soup, without any obvious meat content, at Daquise, the Polish café near the South Kensington Underground station. Cold boiled bacon and sausages are the obvious complements to this soup, whether or not you have omitted stock in making it.

CAULIFLOWER, RED PEPPER AND GINGER SOUP

Devon cauliflowers, 'squeaky-clean' with their curdy, white flowers, are one of the most appealing sights on English vegetable stalls in deep winter. Older people may still serve them in white sauce as an accompaniment to roast lamb, which is a reassuringly bland and sometimes delicate way of presenting them. Younger, that is middle-aged and younger, cooks reared on this side of the post-war Garlic Divide may look for ways of making them taste of something other than plain cauliflower. There is the tomato-sauce option, as in Cauliflower Roman Style (see Jocasta Innes, *The Pauper's Cookbook*, 1971). There is the stir-fry option, in which small cauliflower florets go very well with chopped onion, red pepper, broccoli, cabbage, crushed root ginger and garlic with a final dash of *shoyu* once the vegetables have softened. Also the option, which I have suggested under Green Pea Soup with Meat Juice on p. 37, of mashing cooked cauliflower into the juices of pot-roasted lamb with roast garlic. Then there is soup. In this autumnal recipe, the ginger transforms the cauliflower with a faint taste of chestnuts.

1 medium to large cauliflower	*2 tomatoes, skinned and chopped*
2 onions, peeled and chopped	*2 large cloves garlic, peeled*
1 large red pepper, de-seeded and	*2 thimble-sized pieces ginger root,*
chopped	*peeled and chopped*
2 tablespoons olive oil	*sea salt*
2 potatoes, unpeeled, scrubbed and	*1.2 litres/2 pints water*
diced	

Rinse the cauliflower and divide the white part into florets, discarding the base and leaves. Soften the onions and the pepper in 2 tablespoons of olive oil in a heavy, covered pan. After 10 minutes add the cauliflower and stir it in well. Continue softening for 5–10 minutes more, then add the potatoes, the tomatoes and the garlic and ginger, crushed together in a mortar with a little sea salt. Cook together uncovered, breaking up the tomatoes, then cover with the water, bring to the boil, add 1 teaspoon of sea salt and simmer for 20–30 minutes before liquidizing.

Cauliflower, Spinach and Ginger Soup

A lovely, savoury soup, in which the lively taste of ginger unites the flavours of cauliflower and spinach. Because the texture of cauliflower is always slightly rough, spinach is the best possible vegetable to combine with it for smoothness. Beware, again, of the thick-ribbed, large-leafed chard, which is usually labelled 'spinach' in the shops but would be too harsh and coarse to include in this or indeed in most other kinds of soup demanding spinach.

2 onions, peeled and chopped	10g/¼ oz ginger root, peeled
3 tablespoons sunflower oil	sea salt
450 g/1 lb white part of cauliflower	freshly ground black pepper
4 tomatoes, skinned and chopped	225 g/½ lb summer spinach
4 cloves garlic, peeled	1.2 litres/2 pints water

Soften the onions in 3 tablespoons of sunflower oil in a large, heavy, covered pan. Stir in first the cauliflower, cut into 16–20 florets, then the tomatoes, then 3 chopped cloves of garlic, then the final clove of garlic crushed in a mortar with the ginger and a little sea salt. Simmer all these gently together with the lid on for 10–15 minutes, then season with 1 teaspoon of sea salt and some freshly ground black pepper. Wash the spinach, discarding any slimy or etiolated leaves, cram it into the pan with the cauliflower and tomato mixture, cover it with the water, bring to the boil and simmer for 20–30 minutes. Allow to cool a little before liquidizing.

CAULIFLOWER AND MUSHROOM SOUP

A lovely, light, sharp yet substantial soup with a satisfying blend of tastes.

*1 large or 2 small onions, peeled and
   chopped*
4–5 tablespoons olive oil
1 medium to large cauliflower
*8–10 cloves garlic, peeled and
   chopped*
1.5 litres / 2½ pints water

1 teaspoon sea salt
450–700 g / 1–1½ lb mushrooms
grated nutmeg
*1 bunch watercress or 1 large handful
   sorrel leaves*
freshly ground black pepper
2 tablespoons shoyu or tamari

Soften the onions in 2–3 tablespoons of olive oil in a heavy, covered pan. Discard the main stalk and leaves of the cauliflower, wash the white part, divide it into florets and add these to the onions. Stir in 3 or 4 of the garlic cloves and leave the vegetables to soften, stirring occasionally, with the lid on, for 10–15 minutes. Cover with the water, add the sea salt, bring to the boil and simmer for another 15–20 minutes.

Meanwhile wash the mushrooms, halve them and stew them in 2 table-spoons of olive oil with the remaining cloves of garlic. When the mush-rooms have given off their liquid, add them to the soup with the garlic and liquid. Grate in a little nutmeg. Wash the watercress, discarding any coarse, black lengths of stem or yellow and slimy leaves, or the sorrel and add this to the soup as well. Continue cooking for a few minutes longer, then remove from the heat, cool a little and liquidize. Season with freshly ground black pepper and *shoyu* or *tamari* before serving.

NOTE
Although watercress is usually easier to come by than sorrel in the shops, use sorrel for this soup if you can, since the extra smoothness and piquancy

which it gives to the soup perfectly balances the combination of cauliflower and mushrooms.

CELERIAC SOUP

This autumnal, earth-coloured, fist-shaped root is not immediately the most alluring-looking object in the vegetable shop. Once, however, you have discovered its strong yet delicate flavour, it can be hard to imagine a winter passing without it. As a solid purée, flavoured with garlic and Parmesan cheese, softened with butter and eaten with chopped ham, it makes a very good light supper dish. As the main ingredient of a soup it needs only the simplest treatment to produce one which is thick, bland yet subtle, with a richer taste than Jerusalem artichoke or celery and a pleasant, fawn to golden colour. Do not leave out the potatoes, since they are necessary to give the right smoothness of texture.

2 onions, peeled and chopped
2 large carrots, peeled and chopped
3 tablespoons olive oil
700 g/1½ lb celeriac (roughly, 1 large celeriac root), peeled and diced

2 potatoes, unpeeled, scrubbed and diced
1.75 litres/3 pints water
2 teaspoons sea salt
12 black peppercorns

Soften the onions and carrots in 3 tablespoons of olive oil in a heavy, covered pan. After 10 minutes add the peeled and diced celeriac and the potatoes and continue softening for another 10 minutes, stirring now and again. Cover with the water, add 2 teaspoons of sea salt and a dozen black peppercorns, bring to the boil and simmer for 30 minutes before liquidizing.

CELERY SOUP

Choosing the right head of celery is more than half the battle in producing a good celery soup. If you can find it, go for the long-stemmed, fiercely green, luxuriant variety, which you are unlikely to find in a supermarket but may come across in a Cypriot greengrocer's and general store. Avoid pale, brittle-looking celery, especially if it has brown patches on the outsides of the stems and etiolated-looking leaves. Whatever the virtues of blanching celery may once have been, this process on a commercial scale now seems to result only in the extinction of almost all flavour. Israeli celery is usually reliable enough, but Spanish and Italian less so. If you find, on breaking open the head of celery, that the outer sticks are swollen into blisters on the inward-facing surface and that they are dry and pithy inside, do not try to make them into soup. If the celery seems very stringy, do not put it through the electric liquidizer; or, if you have done so and the resulting soup is full of unpleasantly stringy bits, push it through a *moulin-légumes* or sieve to exclude them.

This may sound sufficiently off-putting to send you straight to a tin of commercial cream of celery soup; but in fact a simple, home-made celery soup is one of the nicest, if not one of the most reliable, winter foods. It is also much less salty than the tinned kind, which relies heavily on artificial stimulants to the taste-buds.

2 onions, peeled and chopped	1.5 litres / 2½ pints water
2 carrots, peeled and chopped	sea salt
3 tablespoons olive oil	black peppercorns
1 large head of celery	fresh lovage, if available, or fresh
2 potatoes, unpeeled, scrubbed and diced	parsley, chopped

Soften the onions and carrots in 3 tablespoons of olive oil in a heavy, covered pan. Wash and scrape the celery sticks, split the main part of each one vertically and cut it into 2.5 cm/1 in lengths. Stir the celery into the pan and leave it to steam-cook for 20–30 minutes over a low heat to bring out the flavour. Add the washed and diced potatoes, cover with the water, season with just over 1 teaspoon of sea salt and a few black peppercorns, bring to the boil and simmer for 20 minutes. Before liquidizing, add a little chopped lovage, a celery-tasting perennial herb which grows easily in any soil in English gardens. In winter, when fresh lovage is unavailable, substitute chopped parsley.

CHESTNUT SOUP

In October in England, the prickly husks fallen from the sweet chestnut trees too often conceal concave and unusable fruit rather than the well-filled kind which we import from southern Europe. The great chestnuts planted in the late seventeenth century in parks such as those at Greenwich or at Levens in Cumbria, with their twisted, vertically striated trunks, must be valued for their ruined grandeur and for the rich appearance of their long, serrated leaves and thick clusters of fruit husks in late summer rather than for their usefulness as a source of autumnal and winter food. Only after unusually hot summers do English chestnuts produce fruit which are plump enough to roast, or to make into soups or puddings.

All over southern Europe, on the other hand, from the foothills of the Pyrenees to the lower slopes of the Italian Alps and further east, chestnuts have been cultivated as a serious substitute for both wheat flour and meat. In the country markets of the Aveyron and the Ardèche, in late September, they are sold unhusked in baskets among a clutter of dead and live rabbits, guinea-fowl and game, while the first chill wind whirls the fallen plane leaves around the town square. Once regarded by poorer people as a necessary 'filler', comparable with beans or cornmeal in more southerly or flatter areas, they are now simply one among many traditional foods, to be made into soup, a stuffing for poultry or game birds, or the *marrons glacés* and whipped-cream desserts which were formerly luxuries only for the rich. The early seventeenth-century exile, Giacomo Castelvetro, writing on the fruits, herbs and vegetables of Italy for the Countess of Bedford, showed how in his time chestnuts were valued by all classes, and how they ranged from a delicacy cooked in white wine and then smoked, or dried among rose-petals, to the plainly boiled 'main food for thousands in our mountainous regions, who hardly ever see wheat bread'.★ He also commented that sweet chestnuts were non-existent in England; and it would be pleasant to attribute to his influence the widespread planting of chestnut trees both in the early part of that century and in the second great wave of planting after the Restoration.

Chestnut soup was established in England at least by Eliza Acton's time, when it consisted of chestnuts boiled in stock, sieved, and mixed with stock and cream. As chestnuts are naturally sweet, the resulting soup must have tasted extremely rich and bland. Most recipes continue to recommend stock, although I find that *shoyu*, a traditional accompaniment of Chinese chestnuts, does very well to counteract the sweetness and give the soup the necessary savoury taste.

450 g/1 lb chestnuts	1.2 litres/2 pints water
1 large onion, peeled and chopped	1 teaspoon sea salt
2 medium to large carrots, peeled and	2 tablespoons shoyu or tamari
chopped	fresh parsley, chopped (optional)
2 tablespoons olive oil	

Skin the chestnuts. This is done by nicking their skins on either side with the point of a sharp knife and then either boiling them for 5–10 minutes or toasting them for 5 minutes on each side under a hot grill. Take them

★Giacomo Castelvetro, *The Fruit, Herbs and Vegetables of Italy*, translated with an introduction by Gillian Riley (1989), 124–125.

out a few at a time, leaving the others either in the water or under the cooling grill, and remove the hard outer and papery inner skins with the point of the knife. Meanwhile soften the onion and carrots in 2 tablespoons of olive oil in a heavy, covered pan. After 10–15 minutes add the chestnuts to them, cover them with the water, add the sea salt, bring to the boil and simmer for 20–30 minutes. Liquidize and add the *shoyu* or *tamari* to taste. Do not use cheap supermarket soy sauce, as it will completely wreck the flavour. Chopped parsley also goes well sprinkled over this soup.

CHESTNUT AND BROCCOLI SOUP

By the chestnut season, much of the home-grown broccoli in the shops is fit only for soup, while red peppers are often relatively cheap. This is one of the happy accidents of soup making.

450 g / 1 lb chestnuts	*2 tablespoons olive oil*
2 onions, peeled and chopped	*4 cloves garlic, peeled*
2 carrots, peeled and chopped	*sea salt*
1 large red pepper, de-seeded and	*450 g / 1 lb broccoli (calabrese)*
chopped	*1.75 litres / 3 pints water*

Skin the chestnuts as explained in the previous recipe. Soften the onions and carrots in 2 tablespoons of olive oil in a heavy, covered pan. Add the pepper and the garlic, crushed with a little sea salt in a mortar, and continue softening for another 5–10 minutes. Peel the stalks of the broccoli unless these are very tender. Wash and cut up the broccoli and add it with the chestnuts to the contents of the pan. Cover with the water, bring to the boil, simmer for 20 minutes, season with 1–2 teaspoons of sea salt and liquidize.

CHESTNUT AND BROWN LENTIL SOUP

A really solid soup, this. Brown lentil soup, highly popular with the health-conscious since the early 1970s, could be classified, like brown rice, as wholesome but boring. Attempts to liven it up sometimes include tomato or even curry sauce, both of which seem to me to be as wrong with brown lentils as they are right with the softer, split red ones. According to macro-biotic cookery theory, most of the things which go well with brown lentils (onions, cabbage, chestnuts) are *yang*, or calming and good for you, whereas most of those which go well with red lentils (peppers, potatoes, tomatoes) are *yin*, exciting and bad for you. It might be a mistake, both nutritionally and gastronomically, to go very far with this theory; but the pattern in this case does seem to be both consistent and interesting.

Chestnuts, then, are okay with brown lentils; and the texture of tinned chestnut purée, often more convenient and accessible than the real thing, smooths down the slightly monotonous roughness which the skins of the lentils give to a puréed soup.

175 g/6 oz brown lentils

1.2–1.75 litres/2–3 pints water

1 onion, peeled and chopped

2 carrots, peeled and chopped

2 sticks celery, washed and chopped

2 tablespoons olive oil

1 small bunch parsley, chopped

1–2 teaspoons sea salt

1–2 tablespoons shoyu or tamari

175–200 g/6–7 oz tinned chestnut
  purée

Soak the lentils in cold water for an hour, drain them, cover them with about 1.2 litres/2 pints of water in a saucepan, bring them to the boil and cook them fast, uncovered, for 5–10 minutes (a precaution now advised with most forms of dried beans and pulses), then simmer them, covered, for about 1 hour. Do not add salt at this stage. Soften the onion, carrot and celery in 2 tablespoons of olive oil in a heavy, covered pan. When both the vegetables and the lentils are soft, amalgamate them with what remains of the water and simmer them together for another 15–20 minutes, having added enough extra water to cover them (probably about 570 ml/1 pint). Add the chopped parsley, the sea salt and the *shoyu* or *tamari* to taste and liquidize. Then return the soup to the pan and reheat it, stirring in the chestnut purée until the soup is a rich, uniform brown flecked with parsley green.

LEEK AND POTATO SOUP (WINTER VERSION)

The classic *potage bonne femme*, probably the best-known and easiest soup to make at home in the winter. It can be enriched with chicken stock or left plain as you wish, and is very simple to make in large quantities for any kind of gathering from a wedding party to a funeral lunch. If either of these suggestions sounds eccentric, think how often, after standing around in the cold, one would welcome a cup or bowl of real soup rather than the dry white wine, crisps and canapés which are so often thrust on one on such occasions. The soup should freeze well if you have made too much, but is obviously best within a day or two of being made and will not keep for more than about two days in the refrigerator before the leeks and onions begin to go rancid. Elizabeth David (*French Provincial Cooking*, 1970) omits onions from her recipe; I find, however, that they improve the soup, giving it an extra mellowness which it may need if you have inferior leeks.

Opinions vary about the kind of leeks to look for to get the most effective flavour. On the whole it is best to avoid obviously end-of-season leeks with a coarse, yellowish complexion and a thick central core to the stem. Short, stubby ones with very dark green leaves can also taste bitter in comparison with the new, thin, delicate kind. Use the green part with discretion, throwing out any which is dark green and sticking to the milder, greenish-yellow part. This is often the part which gives the soup its most characteristic and delicious taste.

2 onions, peeled and chopped	*900 g/2 lb potatoes, scrubbed and*
2 carrots, peeled and chopped	*diced*
3 tablespoons olive oil	*6–10 black peppercorns*
900 g/2 lb leeks	*1.75 litres/3 pints water*
2 teaspoons sea salt	*fresh parsley, if available*

Soften the onions and carrots in 3 tablespoons of olive oil in a heavy, covered pan. Wash the leeks, discarding the base and the coarsest green parts of each, and slit them lengthways on either side of the stem to release trapped pockets of dirt. Chop them into 2.5 cm/1 in lengths, stir them into the onions and carrots and continue softening for another 10–15 minutes, stirring occasionally. This period can be lengthened quite considerably, say for up to 30 minutes, as leeks produce a great deal of their own juice and benefit from slow stewing. Add the potatoes, the sea salt and the peppercorns, cover with the water, bring to the boil, simmer for 20–30 minutes and liquidize. If you have any fresh parsley, add this just before liquidizing or sprinkle it, finely chopped, on the surface of the soup just before serving.

LEEK AND WATERCRESS SOUP

2 onions, peeled and chopped
3 carrots, peeled and chopped
3 tablespoons olive oil
900 g/2 lb leeks
450 g/1 lb potatoes, scrubbed and
    diced

just over 1.2 litres/2 pints water
2 teaspoons sea salt
6–10 black peppercorns
1 good bunch watercress, cleaned and
    chopped

Make as in the previous recipe, but reduce the amount of water to just over 1.2 litres/2 pints and add the watercress 5–10 minutes before liquidizing. A delicate, smooth, green soup.

POTATO, OLIVE AND ANCHOVY SOUP

A useful store-cupboard soup if you have run out of fresh supplies, since you can use both tinned anchovies and tinned olives. Plenty of good extra virgin olive oil is essential with this soup.

2 onions, peeled and chopped

3 tablespoons extra virgin olive oil

900 g/2 lb red-skinned potatoes, scrubbed

1.75 litres/3 pints water

110 g/4 oz black olives, stoned

12 anchovy fillets

Soften the onions in 2 tablespoons of olive oil in a heavy, covered pan. Cut up the potatoes into quarters and boil them in 1.75 litres/3 pints of water until they are just soft. Drain them, reserving the potato water, and cut them up into smallish pieces. Add another tablespoon of oil to the onions, then add the potatoes. Stir, adding as you do so the olives and the anchovy fillets, and allow the flavours to become well mingled. Pitted olives are more tasteless than the kind with their stones in them, so it is worth spending a little extra time stoning your own olives by hand if you have the patience to do so. Add the potato water, bring to the boil and simmer for 5–10 minutes before liquidizing.

A smooth, pleasant, slightly gravy-like soup with an unusual, piquant flavour. Good with cold meat and a sharp salad for contrast, perhaps of young sorrel leaves and Florentine fennel.

CREAM OF SALSIFY AND MUSHROOM SOUP

Salsify is the long, thin, darkly earth-coloured root which can be found in greengrocers' shops in February. When scrubbed, it is revealed to be white without an obvious outer skin; and when punctured, it oozes small quantities of a sticky, white juice. Once highly regarded as a delicacy, it was known in Victorian England as the 'vegetable oyster'. Dorothy Hartley (*Food in England*, 1954) referred to its 'curiously salt, fishy flavour', and maintained that it was 'so like oyster that it takes in the cat!'. André Simon's *Guide to Good Food and Wines* (1963), declared that salsify 'must have lost' any oyster flavour which had previously been associated with it, 'but . . . is none the less one of the best winter vegetables'. I find salsify bland but pleasant, certainly not salty or oyster-flavoured. In soup it demands gentle treatment with quiet, harmonious accompaniments to bring out the delicacy of its flavour.

450 g/1 lb salsify	*1.2 litres/2 pints water*
2 onions	*25 g/1 oz butter*
2–3 tablespoons sunflower oil	*25 g/1 oz flour*
275 g/10 oz mushrooms, cleaned	*150 ml/¼ pint milk*
and roughly chopped	*sea salt*
1 tablespoon olive oil	*freshly ground black pepper*

Scrub the salsify in plenty of water, discard the ends of the roots and cut the rest into 1 cm/½ in lengths. Peel and chop the onions and soften them with the salsify for 10–15 minutes in 2–3 tablespoons of sunflower oil in a heavy, covered pan. Old-fashioned recipes for salsify as a solid vegetable advise boiling first, then frying; but the reverse of that process works equally well for soup. Stir occasionally to prevent sticking, as salsify is dry.

Meanwhile stew the mushrooms in 1 tablespoon of olive oil until they have given off their liquid, reserve the liquid and add the mushrooms to the salsify and onion. Cover with the water, bring to the boil and simmer for 20 minutes. In a heavy pan, melt the butter, stir in the flour and gradually add first the mushroom-liquid, then the milk. When you have a thick sauce, slowly stir in the liquid from the soup, add the vegetables and liquidize. Season with sea salt and freshly ground black pepper to taste.

Spinach and Red Pepper Soup

Strictly, spinach should perhaps count as a summer, not a winter soup vegetable, since I exclude from it spinach beet or chard, that thick-stemmed, coarse-leaved, all-year substitute which is so often misleadingly labelled 'spinach'. In summer, however, it would be a waste of the fine texture and delicate flavour of home-grown spinach to immerse it in soup. The best kind to make into soup is the imported Italian spinach which is available in plastic bags in supermarkets or loose on market stalls throughout the winter.

In its simplest form spinach soup is one of the archetypal foods of the Russian in exile. More than twenty years ago, I had an elderly Russian teacher on the Upper West Side of New York who ate little else. Ill, alone in the world, in his seventies (he had been a student at the University of Petrograd at the time of the Revolution), he did his shopping in a local supermarket where once or twice I met him buying a small, square packet of frozen spinach and a pot of plain yoghurt. These were for spinach soup. Its importance seemed to be partly nostalgic, evoking a vanished way of cooking, a vanished generosity and closeness to nature. Perhaps it helped to re-create for him the atmosphere of Chekhov's short stories which caused him such sadness when we read them together.

Spinach will recur in soups in other sections of this book, as it is a very versatile vegetable which not only curries well but mixes well with a number of other ingredients, from potatoes, peppers and garlic to lentils, meatballs, fish, mussels and prawns. The juicy softness of cooked red peppers goes especially well with the dark green, liquid softness of spinach.

3 large red peppers, de-seeded and chopped	sea salt
2 tablespoons olive oil	6 large cloves garlic, peeled
900 g/2 lb spinach	1 litre/just under 2 pints water
	450 g/1 lb Greek strained yoghurt

Soften the peppers for 10 minutes in 2 tablespoons of olive oil in a heavy, covered pan. Wash the spinach in 2 or 3 changes of water, lifting it straight from the last wash into the pan so that it keeps some water on its leaves, and boil it for about 5 minutes until it has softened and given off some liquid. Season it with 1 teaspoon of sea salt. Crush the garlic with a little more sea salt and add it to the peppers, stirring it well round, then add the spinach with its juices. Cover with the water, bring to the boil and simmer for 10–15 minutes. Liquidize, return to the warm pan and add the yoghurt just before serving.

NOTE

Spinach used to be regarded as a super-healthy vegetable because of its much-vaunted iron content. Now it is recognized that oxalic acid, which is present in most kinds of spinach, makes the iron unavailable for conversion in the human system. Spinach is still, however, high in calcium, although not as high as spinach beet, turnip tops and some other greens. It also has a delicious texture and taste, and has acquired long associations with cheese and egg in such dishes as *spanakopitta* (Greek spinach pie) and *oeufs Florentine* (eggs in cheese sauce with spinach), as well as being a vital

ingredient of minestrone. In northern Indian cookery it combines with
buffalo-milk cheese or with lentils to make curry; and in Russian and
Middle Eastern cookery it is a favourite ingredient of soup. The flexibility
of this classic vegetable must be one reason for its almost worldwide popularity; and it is always open to experimentation by soup-makers and others.

SPINACH SOUP WITH SPLIT PEAS

A soup inspired by Claudia Roden's *A Book of Middle Eastern Food* (1970),
which includes both lentil and spinach soup and yellow split pea soup with
cumin and lemon. Spinach is a natural partner to many pulses, and is
served with them, either separately or together, all over the Middle East
and as far as north-western India.

450 g / 1 lb yellow split peas   *sea salt*
1.75 litres / 3 pints water   *8 cloves garlic, peeled*
2 onions   *25 g / 1 oz butter*
2 tablespoons olive oil   *juice of 1 lemon*
900 g / 2 lb spinach

Soak the split peas for 1–2 hours, or overnight if they have been in your
store cupboard for a long time. Allow just over 1 hour for making the
soup, half of which will be devoted to boiling the split peas until they are
soft. When doing this, cover them with 1.75 litres/3 pints of unsalted
water, bring them to the boil and cook them uncovered at a rapid gallop
for 5–10 minutes, before lowering the heat to simmering-point and cover-

ing the pan. (This is a precaution now advised with most forms of dried beans and peas.) After 30 minutes, peel and chop the onions and begin to soften them in 2 tablespoons of olive oil in a heavy, covered pan. Wash the spinach in 3 changes of water, boil it in the water remaining on the leaves from the last rinse, with a little sea salt, for 10 minutes, drain it, and stir in the garlic crushed with a little sea salt. If you are keen on spinach water, reserve this in case the soup needs diluting later. Add the spinach and garlic to the onions, stir in the butter, squeeze on the lemon juice, then pour on the split peas with their remaining water and add 1–2 teaspoons of sea salt. Simmer all together for 15 minutes, then liquidize.

Spinach and Tomato Soup

A highly garlicky soup with a velvety spinach background.

2 onions, peeled and chopped	freshly ground black pepper
2 tablespoons olive oil	pinch of sugar (optional)
450 g / 1 lb tomatoes, skinned and	900 g / 2 lb spinach
chopped	1 litre / just under 2 pints water
8 cloves garlic, peeled	fried bread croûtons, to serve
sea salt	(see p. 31)
1 tablespoon fresh thyme or basil	fresh basil (optional)

Soften the onions in 2 tablespoons of olive oil in a heavy, covered pan. After 10–15 minutes add the tomatoes, the garlic crushed in a mortar with a little sea salt, and 1 tablespoon of thyme leaves. (If using basil, add it at the end of cooking, unless it has been frozen.) Cook uncovered, breaking up the tomatoes as if for a sauce, until they have disintegrated, and season with salt, pepper and a little sugar if necessary. Meanwhile wash the spinach as in the previous recipe and boil it for 5–10 minutes in its own water with a little sea salt. Add the spinach with its juices to the tomato sauce, cover with the water, bring to the boil and simmer for 10–15 minutes before liquidizing.

Serve with fried bread croûtons and a sprinkling of chopped fresh basil if you have any to hand.

SOUPS USING AVOCADO PEAR

Like roast garlic, the subject of my next section, the blended-in flesh of avocado pear provides an excellent background taste and texture in soups. And not only chilled soups, that favourite feature of magazine articles about summer dinner-party food, but proper, warming soups, suitable for family consumption on an autumn or winter evening. Avocado pear marries well with a number of other tastes, from red pepper and tomato to chestnut or mussel. The idea of cooking avocado pears may seem repellent to some, especially if they have been reared on the idea that the avocado must keep its essential integrity and may be dressed, but never mixed, with only a little olive oil, lemon juice and garlic or perhaps a few prawns in mayonnaise. Sadly, however, not all avocado pears on the market are fit to be presented in this way. Some may turn out to be underripe or blandly tasteless when you cut them open; others, too strongly yellow or patchily discoloured. There is no need to throw these away when they can often be improved by gentle warming and mixing into a sympathetic soup or into a warm winter salad with plenty of garlic, tomato, cubes of bread soaked in extra virgin olive oil and fresh herbs. The secret is not to cook the avocado pears too thoroughly, but simply to chop each half into several pieces after removing the skin and to warm the pieces through for the minimum time necessary to allow their flavour to blend with those of the other ingredients.

AVOCADO, PEPPER AND TOMATO SOUP

Onions are unnecessary to give sweetness to this soup, as the red and yellow peppers contain enough sweetness of their own.

2 large red or yellow peppers, or
*   1 of each*
2 tablespoons olive oil
450 g / 1 lb tomatoes
sea salt
freshly ground black pepper

3–4 cloves garlic, peeled
1 tablespoon fresh thyme and / or
*   marjoram*
1.2 litres / 2 pints water
2 large or 4 small avocado pears

De-seed, wash and chop the peppers and cook them gently for 10–15 minutes in 2 tablespoons of olive oil in a heavy, covered pan. Stir them every now and again to make sure that they do not brown except at the edges. Peel and roughly chop the tomatoes and add them to the peppers with 1 teaspoon of sea salt, some freshly ground black pepper, the garlic, either chopped or crushed in a mortar with a little sea salt, and 1 tablespoon of fresh thyme and/or marjoram leaves. Cook uncovered for 5–10 minutes over a higher heat, breaking up the tomatoes as if for a sauce. Cover with the water, bring to the boil and simmer, covered, for 10–15 minutes. Then peel and stone the avocado pears, discarding any bad bits, chop them roughly and add them to the soup, simmering it for a moment or two longer until they have just warmed through. Liquidize and serve, perhaps with a creamy cheese such as Vignotte and a plain salad of watercress, which should contrast well with this smooth, reddish-golden soup.

Avocado, Duck and Orange Soup

Now that small, lean ducks, such as Sainsburys' French-reared Barbary ducks, are readily available and cost no more, pound for pound, than free-range chickens, duck stock can be one of the major assets of the soup kitchen. Darker, richer and fuller in taste than chicken stock, it makes a perfect background to delicate vegetables whose taste needs bringing out: among them, celery, mangetout peas and avocado pears. In this soup the acidity of freshly squeezed orange juice, a traditional means of cutting through the fatty taste of old-fashioned farmyard duck, provides a welcome contrast to the blandness of the avocado pear.

1 large onion, peeled and chopped
2 tablespoons olive oil
2 large carrots, peeled and chopped
3 sticks celery, chopped
1.2 litres/2 pints duck stock
2 large avocado pears

2 large cloves garlic, peeled
sea salt
juice of 1 large orange
freshly ground black pepper
1 tablespoon extra virgin olive oil

Gently soften the onion in 2 tablespoons of olive oil in a heavy, covered pan. After 5 minutes add the carrots and celery and continue softening for another 10–15 minutes. Pour on the stock (which should ideally have been made several hours earlier, refrigerated and skimmed) and bring to the boil. Simmer, covered, for 25–30 minutes with the lid on. Halve the avocado pears, peel the halves and discard the stones, then cut the flesh into rough chunks in a bowl. Crush the garlic cloves in a mortar with a little sea salt, then mash them into the avocado flesh with the orange juice, some freshly ground black pepper and the extra virgin olive oil. Add a teaspoon of sea salt if the stock is unseasoned. Turn off the heat under the soup, add the avocado mixture and leave it for 10 minutes for the avocado to warm through, then cool a little. Liquidize and serve at room temperature.

A rich, light soup.

Avocado and Walnut Soup

I occasionally have cravings for walnuts as a source of non-meat protein, especially in early spring when Lenten abstinence confirms the age-old ritual of eschewing meat to purify the blood. Walnut sandwiches; carrot and walnut salad; walnut soups: all these, for a time, assuage the longing for simple, nourishing, clean-tasting food. This soup is one which requires chicken stock and soy sauce to pull the flavours together. It improves with age and has a delicate colour and an interestingly rugged texture.

1 large onion, peeled and chopped
2 tablespoons olive oil
175 g/6 oz shelled walnuts
4 large cloves garlic, peeled
sea salt

1.2 litres/2 pints chicken stock
3 large avocado pears
2–3 tablespoons shoyu or tamari
4 tablespoons Greek strained yoghurt

Gently soften the onion for 10–15 minutes in 2 tablespoons of olive oil in a heavy, covered pan. Break up the walnuts; crush the garlic in a mortar with a little sea salt, and pound the walnuts and garlic together until you have a paste. Add this to the onion, pour on the strained and skimmed stock, bring to the boil and simmer, covered for 20–25 minutes. Halve the avocado pears, discard the stones, peel the halves and cut the flesh into chunks. Turn the heat off under the soup, add the avocado pear chunks and leave to stand for 5–10 minutes. Liquidize, stir in the *shoyu* or *tamari* and the yoghurt, adjust the seasoning and serve.

AVOCADO, SPINACH AND SORREL SOUP

A lovely, green soup for people with that useful, perennial clump of sorrel in their gardens, which dies down in the late autumn but is already pushing up fresh, sharp-tasting new leaves by the beginning of March. The avocado pear forms a liaison between the rougher-textured spinach (which may be chard, otherwise spinach beet, in this soup) and the smoother, more piquant sorrel. If sorrel is omitted the spinach should be real spinach, not chard; but the soup, although pleasant, may be a little too bland.

2 onions, peeled and chopped	*sea salt*
2 tablespoons olive oil	*4–6 cloves garlic, peeled*
900 g/2 lb spinach	*2 handfuls sorrel leaves*
850 ml/1½ pints water	*2 avocado pears*

Soften the onions in 2 tablespoons of olive oil in a heavy, covered pan. Meanwhile wash the spinach thoroughly in 3 changes of water, discarding any slimy or etiolated leaves, and tear it up roughly if the leaves are big. Add the spinach to the softened onions, raise the heat a little and cook it quite fast for 5–10 minutes with the lid on until it has begun to give off a bubbling liquid. Add the water with 1 teaspoon of sea salt, bring this to the boil and simmer it, covered, for about 15 minutes. Crush the garlic with half a teaspoon of sea salt; wash and tear up the sorrel leaves; peel and stone the avocado pears. Add these 3 ingredients to the soup in the order given, bearing in mind that sorrel cooks almost instantaneously and that the avocado pears must do no more than just warm through. Turn off the heat and leave the soup to stand for a few minutes before liquidizing.

Avocado and Mussel Soup

Mussels are not to everybody's taste. Increasing fears of polluted mussel beds have added one more argument to the many advanced by people who 'never touch shellfish'. Yet mussels, it seems, are less vulnerable to pollution than oysters, and may indeed come to replace them if the East Anglian oyster beds are forced to close down. In France they have always been more highly prized than they are here, and give a strong, distinctive taste to many seaside fish soups from Normandy to the Mediterranean. This taste comes chiefly from the abundant liquid which they give off when gently cooked in a heavy, covered pan, and which makes them an especially good ingredient in soups. If you dislike the idea of their texture, you can simply liquidize them with the rest of the soup or (in extreme cases) leave them out and use only their juices. The main criteria for safety are these: if a mussel is already open when you buy it, or opens in cold water while being washed, it should be discarded. Similarly, any mussels which refuse to open after steaming should be discarded. All others are almost certain to be safe except for people with allergies, which is another story altogether.

---

900 g/2 lb mussels

2 medium to large onions, peeled and
   chopped

4 small or 2 large red or green/orange
   peppers, de-seeded and chopped

3 tablespoons olive oil

450 g/1 lb tomatoes

6–8 cloves garlic, peeled

sea salt

freshly ground black pepper

fresh marjoram (optional)

2 avocado pears

850 ml–1.2 litres/1½–2 pints water

Clean the mussels in a sinkful of cold water, scrubbing and rinsing their shells and tugging off the loose strands known as the 'beard'. Soften the onions and peppers in 3 tablespoons of olive oil in a heavy, covered pan for 10–15 minutes. Skin and roughly chop the tomatoes, crush the garlic in a mortar with a little sea salt and add these to the onions and peppers. Cook uncovered as if for a sauce, breaking up the tomatoes and adding sea salt, freshly ground black pepper and a little fresh marjoram, if you have it.

Add the mussels in their shells, replace the lid and leave the mussels to exude their juices for 15 minutes. Then remove the mussels with a slotted spoon and keep them warm while you peel and stone the avocado pears, cut them into several pieces each and add them to the soup to warm through. At this stage you may shell the mussels one by one into the pan and liquidize them with the rest of the ingredients of the soup; or you may reserve them until after liquidizing and add them at that stage, last of all. Pour on 850 ml–1.2 litres/1½–2 pints water until the other ingredients are covered; add a pinch of sea salt; bring to the boil, cool a little and liquidize.

Served with plenty of good wholemeal or granary bread and a creamy cheese, this makes a light supper in itself.

SOUPS USING
ROAST GARLIC

Large cloves of garlic, roasted either alone or with meat to a condition of soft, near-caramelized pungency, have become a commonplace of progressive English cooking during the last twenty years or so. Before that, garlic cloves were always small, perhaps because the growers and exporters were well aware of the English terror of over-garlicked food and deliberately sent us heads of garlic with minuscule cloves, assuming that there would be no market for bigger ones. Now all that has changed. Garlic sold in cardboard cartons in supermarkets is usually of the old-fashioned, unsatisfying variety; but many ethnic shops, greengrocers and even supermarkets with extensive fresh-vegetable sections, such as Sainsburys, sell large, rugged heads of garlic with big, solid cloves, sometimes as few as six or eight to the head.

Attitudes towards garlic are also changing, from a fastidious fear of breathing garlicky fumes in the direction of those who might find them offensive to a positive recognition that garlic can be both delicious and useful as a protective food reducing the risk of coronary heart disease. Nor is there any need to eat it in pill form unless you positively hate its natural taste. Garlic is at its most pungent raw, which accounts for all those recipes instructing the cook to rub the salad bowl with a clove of garlic, then hurl the garlic down the waste-disposal unit and thoroughly wash her hands. Fried, with meat, it can also be heavy on the breath, since this is one of the more indigestible ways of eating it. Roasted, like parsnips, it loses all its crudeness and almost melts within while becoming chewily sweet on the outside. The intensity of its flavour in this state is almost smoky, or reminiscent of the smell of old-fashioned steam trains. Roast garlic, parsnips and small onions are a heavenly mixture, making it almost unnecessary to eat the accompanying meat. As a background to soup, roast garlic cloves are both powerfully flavoured and smooth. It is more conventional, perhaps, to present the garlic as a solid purée; but I happen to like it in combinations of other flavours, and hope that my taste for it in soup is one which may be more widely shared.

ROAST GARLIC SOUP WITH TOMATO

In nearly all the traditional recipes for garlic soup, from the simplest Spanish or southern French version (garlic, salt, water, oil, bread) to the more elaborate ones thickened with egg yolks, tomatoes or potatoes and diluted with stock or milk, the preliminary softening of the garlic consists of frying it in the pan in which the soup is to be cooked on top of the stove. The reasons for this are obvious. Soup is the classic 'one-pot' meal, a refinement of those medieval peasant dishes which consisted of meat or vegetables simmered slowly in water in the household's single cooking-pot over an open fire. With the advent of cooking-stoves and the proliferation of kitchen utensils, cooks developed the practice of pre-cooking some or all of the vegetables for soup in butter or oil before immersing them in water. Garlic, therefore, had to be pre-fried, a process which can quickly lead to browning and can intensify its flavour in an unpleasant way. Roast garlic soups develop the idea of a garlic purée which can be made independently of the frying process and has a stronger yet more subtle flavour. Unless you have a solid-fuel cooker or a modern stove with a small, subsidiary oven in addition to the main one, it may seem wasteful to heat up the oven simply for a small dish of garlic cloves. I use a small, worktop electric oven which heats very quickly and can also be used for baking small pies or heating breakfast rolls.

If the thought of peeling 80 cloves of garlic is too much for you, this soup can be made in half-quantities to feed 2 or 3 people as a first course. It is not recommended for freezing or long-term storage.

8 heads of large-cloved garlic, totalling
   70–80 cloves in all
2 tablespoons olive oil
225–275 g/8–10 oz home-made
   wholemeal or granary bread,
   slightly stale

900 g/2 lb tomatoes
75 g/3 oz butter
sea salt
freshly ground black pepper
1.2 litres/2 pints water

Separate the garlic cloves, peel them and put them in a shallow, ovenproof dish with 2 tablespoons of olive oil. Roast them in a medium to hot oven, 200°C, 400°F, gas mark 6, for 15–20 minutes, turning them over once towards the end, until they are beginning to change colour but are not yet a deep, burnt brown. When the garlic is nearly roasted, make room for the bread in the roasting-dish or tin to allow it to crisp up and absorb as much as possible of the garlic-flavoured oil.

Meanwhile, skin the tomatoes by plunging them into just-boiled water, chop them roughly and put them on their own in a covered pan to heat up over a gentle heat for 5–10 minutes. Gradually add the butter and stir this into the tomato juices once they have begun to run. Season with salt and freshly ground black pepper; add the garlic cloves and their residual oil; crumble in the bread and cover with the water. Bring this to the boil and simmer it for 5–10 minutes before liquidizing.

Although tomato-based, this reddish-orange soup is quite unlike a tomato soup, since its prevailing taste is the strong yet surprisingly gentle one of puréed roasted garlic.

ROAST GARLIC SOUP WITH CARROT AND ROSEMARY-FLAVOURED CHICKEN JELLY

A delicious soup to accompany cold roast chicken, as well as a way of using up the cooking juices. For this quantity of soup you will need a fairly big, juicy chicken weighing 1.35–1.8 kg/3–4 lb or more. For half the quantity you can use a 1–1.35 kg/2–3 lb chicken. The garlic for the soup is roasted round the chicken, ideally with a few extra cloves so that you can have the pleasure of eating at least some of them fresh and hot.

FOR THE CHICKEN JELLY
1.35–1.8 kg/3–4 lb roasting chicken
2–3 tablespoons olive oil
1 sprig rosemary
20 large garlic cloves

FOR THE SOUP
6 large carrots, peeled
1.2–1.75 litres/2–3 pints water
sea salt
jelly from the roast chicken (see below)
1 sprig lovage, if in season
freshly ground black pepper

The day before making the soup, roast the chicken in 2 or 3 tablespoons of good olive oil, placing the sprig of rosemary underneath it to transmit its flavour with that of the chicken juices to the oil. About halfway through the roasting time (which should be an hour for a smaller chicken and 1¼ –1½ hours for a bigger one, in a hot oven, 200–220°C, 400–425°F, gas mark 6–7), peel the garlic cloves and arrange them round the chicken. If you follow the precept of roasting the chicken first on one flank, then on the other, you will find that there is usually plenty of room around the chicken, or at least more than when it is roasted straightforwardly breast-upwards. When the chicken is cooked and the cloves of garlic are soft and golden-brown, pour off the juices and garlic into a bowl and refrigerate them overnight.

To begin the soup, cut the carrots into rings about 1 cm/½ in thick, cover them with 1.2 litres/2 pints of water, add a little sea salt and boil them for 10–15 minutes until they are soft. Skim off most of the oil which will have gathered on top of the bowl of chicken juices and garlic and you should find the garlic cloves embedded in a layer of translucent jelly. Heat up the garlic and chicken jelly in a heavy-bottomed pan. Add the cooked carrots and their water, with a sprig of lovage (a strong, celery-tasting perennial herb) if you can get it. For a richer soup, sauté the drained carrots in some of the oil from the chicken before adding them to the soup. This may increase your intake of fat, but also helps to release the carotene and Vitamin A in the carrots during digestion. Liquidize the soup, add a further 520 ml/1 pint or so of water if it seems too thick, season with a pinch of sea salt and some freshly ground black pepper and reheat to serve. This frothy, pinkish-orange soup should not be served boiling hot, but it is very good warm, allowing the various flavours to emerge.

ROAST GARLIC SOUP WITH RED CABBAGE AND PARSNIPS

Red cabbage is not the easiest vegetable to turn into soup, as it needs both flavouring and long, slow cooking to bring out the best in it. Liquidized, it can resemble an unappetizing mauve porridge. If well seasoned, however, against a thick, sweetish background of roast garlic and parsnips, it can make a lovely, filling soup which is a meal in itself.

450 g / 1 lb red cabbage

4 tablespoons olive oil

12–15 large cloves garlic, peeled

sea salt

1 large chilli pepper, de-seeded

4 tomatoes, skinned and chopped

1 glass red wine

1.5 litres / 2½ pints water

450 g / 1 lb parsnips

Rinse the cabbage under the cold tap, remove the base and any wilted outer leaves and shred the rest as finely as you can. Heat 2 tablespoons of the oil in a heavy, lidded pan and stir in the cabbage, turning down the heat as cabbage burns easily. Crush a couple of the cloves of garlic with a little sea salt and add these to the cabbage with the very finely chopped chilli. Leave these to soften, covered, stirring them occasionally, for 10–15 minutes, then add the tomatoes, the wine and a large pinch of sea salt. Replace the lid and continue simmering for 10 minutes, giving an occasional stir to break up the tomatoes, until the cabbage has become an aromatic, purple mush. Cover with the water, bring to the boil and simmer for 20–30 minutes.

Meanwhile peel the parsnips, halve or slice them lengthways depending on their size, blanch them for a moment or two in boiling, lightly salted water (to which you may add the garlic cloves if these are very large), then roast the remaining garlic cloves and parsnips together in 2 tablespoons of olive oil in a medium to hot oven, 200°C, 400°F, gas mark 6, for 20 minutes. When they are golden brown and soft, but not brown or chewy, put them in the liquidizer with the liquid from the soup, reserving the cabbage, and blend them together. Reunite the thickened liquid with the cabbage, simmer for a moment over a gentle heat, then cool a little and serve.

Good with wholemeal or granary bread, a chunky pâté or slices of Continental sausage.

Roast Garlic Soup with Lovage and Celery

This is a spring soup for lovage-lovers, who enjoy the slightly peppery taste and celery-like scent of this tall, clump-forming, perennial herb. I have never seen lovage for sale in greengrocers' shops or on delicatessen counters; but it grows very easily, recurring year after year. Every spring I try to find excuses to cook with it and to use the tender, aromatic new leaves before they coarsen and become dull.

2–3 carrots, peeled and chopped

3 tablespoons olive oil

10–12 large cloves garlic, peeled

1 large head celery

3–4 potatoes, scrubbed and diced

1.2 litres / 2 pints water

1 teaspoon sea salt

6 black peppercorns or freshly ground
*   black pepper*

2–3 tablespoons fresh lovage leaves

Soften the carrots in 2 tablespoons of the olive oil in a heavy, covered pan. Put on the whole garlic cloves to roast in another spoonful of oil in a moderately hot oven, 190°C, 375°F, gas mark 5. Wash, trim and chop the celery and stir it into the carrots, leaving it to cook in its own steam for 15–20 minutes. Add the softened garlic cloves with their oil and the scrubbed and diced, but unpeeled potatoes; cover with the water; season with the sea salt and a twist of black pepper or half a dozen black peppercorns; bring to the boil and simmer for 20 minutes before liquidizing. Add the lovage during the simmering process, adjusting the amount to the strength of taste which you think will be acceptable in the soup. Three tablespoons of leaves give a very strong, peppery taste and a bright green, flecked effect; but the taste becomes modified on reheating, and has by then had time to blend with the almost equally powerful flavour of the roast garlic.

CELERY AND ROAST GARLIC SOUP

Omitting the lovage, but adding an onion, this soup can also be made as an unsophisticated, earthy-tasting celery and roast garlic soup, which is a good way of saving a rather characterless head of celery if it will not stand up to being made into celery soup in the more conventional way.

ROAST GARLIC AND POTATO SOUP

The harmonious marriage of potatoes and garlic can be seen in the best kind of potato pancakes, and also in the Greek form of mayonnaise, *skordalia*. In some versions this is made using olive oil, garlic, egg yolks, ground almonds and breadcrumbs; in others, simply boiled, mashed potatoes, garlic and olive oil.* The French *aioli*, made with olive oil, garlic and egg yolks, is customarily eaten with a dish of plainly boiled potatoes in addition to other vegetables. Roast garlic and roast potatoes together make a wonderful accompaniment to small helpings of roast beef, lamb or chicken; while roast garlic blended with boiled potatoes, as it is in this soup, has a pungent, sweetish taste and a calming texture.

30–40 large cloves garlic (4–5 large heads)	*700 g / 1½ lb potatoes*
2–3 tablespoons extra virgin olive oil	*1.5 litres / 2½ pints water*
1 onion	*1 teaspoon sea salt*
2 carrots	*freshly ground black pepper*

*For the latter version, see, for example, James Chatto and W.L. Martin, *A Kitchen in Corfu* (1987).

Peel the cloves of garlic and roast them in 1 tablespoon of the olive oil in a moderately hot oven, 190°C, 375°F, gas mark 5, for 15–20 minutes, until they are just golden and soft but not brown. Peel and quarter the onion, peel and slice the carrots, scrub (but do not peel) the potatoes and cut them into 2.5 cm/1 in thick cubes. Boil all these together for about 15 minutes in the water with 1 teaspoon of sea salt until the carrots and potatoes are soft. Add the roast garlic cloves and their residual oil to the vegetables, cool slightly and liquidize. Season with freshly ground black pepper and stir another 1–2 tablespoons of extra virgin olive oil into the smooth, pale brown soup before serving.

ROAST GARLIC SOUP WITH BLACK-EYED BEANS AND PARSLEY

Bean soups are proverbially heavy, hearty forms of food. Here, however, is an elegant and sophisticated bean soup, in which the beans themselves provide a background to the creamy-textured, subtle-tasting roast garlic and the fresh green colour and taste of the parsley.

225 g/8 oz black-eyed beans	*1 tablespoon olive oil*
1.75 litres/3 pints water	*50–75 g/2–3 oz parsley*
15–20 large cloves garlic	*1½ teaspoons sea salt*

Soak the beans overnight or for several hours. Drain them, cover them with 1.75 litres/3 pints of cold water, bring them to the boil and cook them fast, uncovered, for 5–10 minutes (a precaution now advised with most forms of dried beans and pulses), then simmer them, covered, for about 1½ hours. Towards the end of the cooking time, peel the garlic cloves and roast them for 15–20 minutes in 1 tablespoon of olive oil in a moderate oven, 180–200°C, 350–400°F, gas mark 4–6. Wash the parsley by immersing it stalks upward in a basin of cold water and repeating the process with clean water until all traces of mud and grit have vanished. Chop the parsley, discarding the thicker ends of the stalks, and add, with the garlic in its oil and the sea salt, to the beans in their remaining water. Simmer together for 5 minutes, then turn off the heat and cool for a little in the pan before liquidizing.

ROAST GARLIC SOUP WITH PUMPKIN AND RED PEPPER

One of the chief aesthetic pleasures of soup-making is the brilliant colour of certain soups. This autumnal one is a glowing, reddish orange, flecked with deeper colour from the red pepper. Its texture is soothing; yet the taste is piquant, improving with reheating.

2 heads large-cloved garlic
2 tablespoons olive oil
450 g / 1 lb pumpkin flesh, peeled, de-seeded and cut up
850 ml / 1½ pints water

1 red pepper, de-seeded and chopped
10 g / ¼ oz ginger root, peeled and chopped
sea salt

Roast the peeled garlic cloves in 1 tablespoon of the olive oil in a moderately hot oven, 180–200°C, 350–400°F, gas mark 4–6, for 15–20 minutes until they begin to turn golden. Meanwhile simmer the cut-up pumpkin flesh in the water in a covered saucepan, and gently soften the red pepper in 1 tablespoon of olive oil in another pan. Crush the ginger root in a mortar with a little sea salt and stir it into the red pepper. Add the garlic, pepper, ginger and their oil to the pumpkin and continue simmering for another 10–15 minutes. Season with a teaspoon of sea salt. Leave to stand until slightly cooled, then liquidize.

A good accompaniment to white fish such as the firm-fleshed hoki, with a dish of highly seasoned mashed potato and carrot and perhaps a watercress salad.

Roast Garlic and White Cabbage Soup with Ginger

A potent, creamy soup, perfect for warmth on a cold winter's day, especially if accompanied by good, home-made bread with butter, smoked salmon pieces and a squeeze of lemon. I devised this soup when painting the house on my own during a freezing December, and found it the perfect sustenance when too tired to cook anything else.

2 onions, peeled and chopped	2 potatoes, scrubbed and diced
4 tablespoons sunflower oil	1 teaspoon Chinese five-spice powder
450 g / 1 lb white cabbage, chopped	1 teaspoon sea salt
25 g / 1 oz ginger root, peeled	freshly ground black pepper
8 large cloves garlic	1.5 litres / 2½ pints water

Soften the onions in 3 tablespoons of sunflower oil in a heavy, covered pan. Add the white cabbage and the finely chopped ginger root, and continue cooking gently with the lid on for about 15 minutes while you roast the garlic cloves in another tablespoon of oil in a moderately hot oven, 190°C, 375°F, gas mark 5. Scrub and dice the potatoes and add these to the onions, ginger and cabbage with the softened garlic in its oil, the five-spice powder, the salt and some freshly ground black pepper. Cover with the water, bring to the boil and simmer for 20–30 minutes. Cool a little and liquidize.

The resulting soup will be thick, white and aromatic, with the sweetness of the roast garlic cloves counterbalancing the pungency of cabbage, ginger and the Chinese spice.

CURRIED
SOUPS

Eliza Acton, in her *Modern Cookery for Private Families* (1845), gives a recipe for a 'good vegetable mulligatawny' soup, made with vegetable marrow, onions, cucumbers, 'mild currie powder' and apples 'or . . . tomatas'. Anticipating the modern trend towards curried lentil or vegetable soups, this dispels any idea that the early Victorians knew only one form of curried soup, a fiery mulligatawny made with a boiling hen, mutton or both. It is also simpler, and in general more attractive, than the 'Cucumber Soup, Indian Style' in my 1920s edition of Mrs Beeton, which calls for a cucumber, onions, a calf's brain, butter, egg yolks, mulligatawny paste and cream. Eliza Acton, however, was a noted exponent of delicate, experimental cooking, with much recourse to spices, curry powders and pastes and the more exotic stock-in-trade of Italian warehouses. The integrity of her style of cookery, with its emphasis on the essential taste of her ingredients, made it possible for her to use spices often but sparingly, as a heightener of taste, without over-compensating on butter and egg yolks. Her 'Buchanan Carrot Soup', for example, is both wholesome and delicious, with the kind of zest in its composition which makes one think of other, simple, early nineteenth-century gourmets such as the Revd Sydney Smith. Carrots, stewed in butter then cooked in beef broth and sieved; Patna rice, gently cooked in the soup; and 'fine currie powder', or, for preference, 'a spoonful of *Captain White's* currie-paste'. No cream, no calf's brain, no egg yolks necessary.

Curried soups made in England now are more likely to resemble Eliza Acton's than those of Mrs Beeton re-edited for the last days of the Raj. The main difference is the lack of reliance on stock for modern curried soups (Eliza Acton suggested stock or broth for her vegetable mulligatawny, although she was apparently content with the option of using water), and the greater solidity of modern, liquidized soups in contrast with early nineteenth-century sieved ones. A modern curried bean or lentil soup in fact resembles the traditional North Indian *dal*, a source of protein and flavour to be eaten sparingly with a main course of rice, curried vegetables or bread, rather than the essentially liquid Victorian curried soup, eaten as an appetizer at the beginning of a lunch or dinner of many courses.

Curried soups often improve with reheating and may be frozen, although some of the flavour will then inevitably be lost.

Cold Curried Avocado Soup with Prawns

An elegant, chilled soup, providing a change from the eternal summer evening gazpacho.

350 g / 12 oz prawns in their shells
1.2 litres / 2 pints water
sea salt
1 medium to large onion, peeled and
  chopped
1–2 tablespoons sunflower oil
1 large chilli pepper, de-seeded and
  finely chopped
3 large cloves garlic

1 teaspoon each cumin, coriander and
  cardamom seeds
1 thimble-sized piece ginger root
4 tomatoes, skinned and chopped
dried curry leaves (optional)
4 avocado pears, stoned and peeled
225–275 g / 8–10 oz Greek strained
  yoghurt

Shell and refrigerate the prawns and make a stock with the shells and heads, simmering these in 1.2 litres/2 pints of lightly salted water for half an hour.

Meanwhile make a basic curry sauce as follows. Lightly brown the onion in 1–2 tablespoons of sunflower oil in a heavy, covered pan. Browning improves the flavour and appearance of the curry; blackening ruins it. Stir in the finely chopped chilli. Grind the spices together in a mortar and stir them into the onion and chilli. Peel and chop the garlic and ginger, crush them together in the mortar with a little sea salt and add them to the mixture in the pan. Skin and roughly chop the tomatoes and stir them in, then cook them uncovered, breaking them up with a wooden spoon, until they have formed a pungent curry sauce. At this stage you may add a few dried curry leaves, removing them before liquidizing the soup. Pour on the strained stock, simmer it for 15–20 minutes, then leave it to cool. When it is cold, add the stoned and peeled avocado pears and the yoghurt. Liquidize, chill for an hour and add the peeled and refrigerated prawns before serving.

CURRIED BEAN SOUP

Although it vaguely resembles both American chilli bean soup and the North Indian *chana dal*, curried bean soup has no true cultural or ethnic antecedents. It is one of the marriages of convenience which have evolved in the modern world between the spices of one culture and the bulk food of another. There is no point in attempting subtlety in this soup, or in piously praising it as the time-honoured food of our peasant ancestors. It should bring tears to the eyes and a feeling of warm fullness to the stomach. With good bread and perhaps an avocado pear, it is, needless to say, very much a meal in itself.

275–350 g/10–12 oz dried beans
(red kidney, white haricot, black-
eyed or a mixture), or 2
400 g/14 oz tins of cooked
beans, drained
2 onions, peeled and chopped
1–2 tablespoons sunflower oil
1 large chilli pepper, de-seeded and
finely chopped
12 allspice berries

1 teaspoon each cumin, coriander and
cardamom seeds
4 cloves garlic
1 thimble-sized piece ginger root
sea salt
4 tomatoes or 75–110 g/3–4 oz
tamarind
225 g/8 oz Greek strained yoghurt
1.5 litres/2½ pints water
fresh mint, chopped

If you are using dried beans, soak them overnight or from after breakfast until teatime, then cover them with water to a depth of at least
5 cm/2 in and boil them well for 1½–2 hours without adding salt. Dried
beans should always be boiled fast with the lid off for the first 10 minutes
to eliminate harmful elements, then may be turned down to a steady
simmer. Make a curry sauce as in the previous recipe, but including
crushed allspice berries for greater richness. If possible, use tamarind
instead of tomatoes; for whereas a tomato-based curry suits certain foods
such as avocado pears, the less delicate beans and pulses go better with the
rougher, more authentically curry-tasting tamarind flavour. Tamarind is
available in the form of a concentrated extract, but tastes much better if
you can buy it in a 200 g/7 oz block, dried and pressed together like cooking dates. Cut off your piece of tamarind, immerse it in a cupful of boiling
water, soak and prod it for 5–10 minutes until it has given off its flavour
and acidity into the water, then strain the liquid (rubbing as much of the
tamarind as you can get through a sieve) into the curry sauce. Cook the
sauce for a few minutes until the liquid has evaporated slightly, then add
the drained cooked dried beans or the tinned beans and stir them round
well in the sauce. Add all but 1 tablespoon of the yoghurt and stir well
again; pour on 1.5 litres/2½ pints of water; bring to the boil and simmer
for 15 minutes, then liquidize. Before serving, stir in the remaining spoonful of yoghurt and sprinkle the surface with chopped mint leaves.

CURRIED LENTIL AND SPINACH SOUP WITH CHUTNEY POTATO BALLS

After a poor reception in this country during the austerity years of postwar rationing, when nobody seemed to know how to spice them up enough, lentils made a comeback in the early 1970s with the simultaneous arrival of the Californian-inspired health-food craze and the discovery of Indian vegetarian cooking. Since then, several generations of students have lived on them as a cheap and cheerful, healthier alternative to hamburgers or fish and chips. In the Italian household in which I lived before going to university, in the early 1960s, we ate lentils ceremonially, as a rarity, 'because they are a very ancient food, the food of the Bible,' the father of the family explained to me. Further east and south, we might have had less choice in the matter; for across the Middle East, from Greece to northern India, lentils have remained a staple, life-saving food from biblical times to the present day. When making soup out of them, it is best to disregard those worthy-looking packets of 'soup-mix' on the health-food shelves of supermarkets, in which red lentils, rice, split peas and beans are all jumbled together, regardless of whether they need pre-soaking or not. Lentils are at their best when highly spiced and combined, not with beans or other pulses to make them stodgier, but with meat or vegetables for contrast and butter or yoghurt for smoothness. One example of such a combination is the northern Indian chicken or meat *dhansak*; another, the classic Punjabi dish of a dollop of orange-brown lentils or *dal*, accompanied by another of dark green, spicy or plain spinach, another of buffalo-milk yoghurt and a piece of chapatti or *nan* bread.

This curried soup, using red lentils (for brown do not curry well), combines the essentials of a dish of *dal* and spinach. It may also be made, however, without the spinach and omitting the extra garnish of chutney potato balls, which are quick and easy to make and convert it from a first course into a fairly filling meal.

225 g/8 oz red lentils	*12 allspice berries*
1.75–2.25 litres/3–4 pints water	*4 cloves garlic*
2 onions, peeled and chopped	*1 thimble-sized piece ginger root*
1–2 tablespoons sunflower oil	*4–5 tomatoes or 75–110g/3–4 oz*
1 large chilli pepper, de-seeded and	* tamarind*
* finely chopped*	*225 g/8 oz Greek strained yoghurt*
1 teaspoon each cumin, coriander and	*450 g/1 lb spinach, washed*
* cardamom seeds*	*1–2 teaspoons sea salt*

Pour the lentils on to a plate in two or three instalments and check them over for pieces of grit or other foreign matter. Most packeted lentils are almost entirely grit-free these days, but it is worth looking to be on the safe side. Rinse them in cold water, cover them with 1.75–2.25 litres/ 3–4 pints of water in a large saucepan with a well-fitting lid, bring them carefully to the boil so that they do not froth over, and simmer them, unsalted, for about 30 minutes. Make a curry sauce as in the previous two recipes, including tamarind if you can (but using fresh tomatoes rather than tinned if you cannot). When the lentils have absorbed about half their water, add the curry sauce to them, then stir in the yoghurt and the washed and torn-up spinach leaves. Simmer for another 10–15 minutes, adding more water if the soup seems too thick, season with sea salt and liquidize.

An appetizingly spicy, pinkish-green soup.

CHUTNEY POTATO BALLS

2 floury potatoes	4 tablespoons strong, spicy chutney
2 eggs	(see below)
sea salt	freshly ground black pepper
2–3 tablespoons sunflower oil	flour

Scrub the potatoes and boil them, quartered, in lightly salted water until they are soft but not disintegrating. Beat the eggs and mash them into the drained potato, adding salt and freshly ground pepper to taste, until you have a smooth mixture. Flatten this out on a floured board, adding more flour to the surface of the mixture to make handling easier. Spread half the potato mixture with the chutney, cover it with the other half to form a sandwich, and form this double layer into balls, making them as small as you can and sealing the chutney inside a complete coating of potato. Shallow-fry the balls for a minute or two in very hot sunflower oil, turning them over once or twice to crisp evenly, and drain them on kitchen paper before serving them in or with the soup.

GREEN TOMATO CHUTNEY

This is a fairly flexible chutney. I have given the smallest practicable amount which can be made at any one time; but if you have a glut of green tomatoes it is easy enough to increase the other ingredients in proportion. You may leave out the peppers, the apple and/or the garlic, or use 1 or 2 eating apples instead of the cooking apple. You may also leave out the tamarind; but, if you do, the chutney will be much less dark and deliciously acidic than otherwise. Crushed black peppercorns may be substituted for allspice, or used in addition to it for an extra tang.

2 onions, peeled

4–6 cloves garlic, peeled

1 cooking apple, peeled and cored

1–2 red peppers, de-seeded

1 chilli pepper, de-seeded

900 g/2 lb green tomatoes

1 thimble-sized piece ginger root

40–50 g/1½–2 oz tamarind

6 allspice berries or 6 black peppercorns

110 g/4 oz raisins

1 tablespoon sea salt

700 ml/1¼ pints wine or cider vinegar, either red or white

350 g/12 oz demerara sugar

Chop the onion and garlic, the apple and the peppers and chilli. Roughly chop, but do not bother to skin, the green tomatoes. Peel and finely shred the ginger. Crush the allspice in a mortar. Immerse the tamarind in a cupful of just-boiled water, leave it soaking for 5–10 minutes, stir it well and then strain the liquid, pushing as much of the tamarind pulp through the strainer as you can. Add this liquid to the remaining ingredients of the chutney in a large, heavy-bottomed saucepan. Boil up everything together and cook it steadily over a moderate heat for about 1 hour, stirring occasionally, until it has a jammy consistency. Bottle in clean jars which have been heated in a low oven.

CURRIED MANGETOUT PEA SOUP

Again, a soup for slightly overgrown, flavourful mangetout peas of your own cultivation (they are very easy to grow even in quite heavy, clay soil) rather than for the insipid, imported kind.

2 onions, peeled and chopped

2 carrots, peeled and chopped

2 tablespoons sunflower oil

1 large chilli pepper, de-seeded and
   finely chopped

1 teaspoon each cumin, coriander and
   cardamom seeds

2 large cloves garlic, peeled

1 thimble-sized piece ginger root,
   peeled

sea salt

2 tomatoes, skinned and chopped, or
   40 g/1½ oz tamarind, soaked as
   described on page 100

450 g/1 lb mangetout peas

just over 1.2 litres/2 pints water

50 g/2 oz unsweetened dessiccated
   coconut

110 g/4 oz Greek strained yoghurt

Soften the onions and carrots in 2 tablespoons of sunflower oil in a heavy, covered pan. After 10 minutes add the finely chopped chilli pepper and stir it well in; then, after a few minutes longer, add the cumin, coriander and cardamom seeds, crushed together finely in a mortar, then the garlic and ginger root, crushed together with a little sea salt to take up the juices, and lastly the tomatoes or the steeped and strained tamarind. Cook all these together uncovered for 5–10 minutes as if for a sauce, while top-and-tailing, de-stringing and roughly chopping up the mangetout peas. Add the peas, cover with the water, bring to the boil and simmer for about 15 minutes. Season with 1 teaspoon of sea salt, add the coconut and yoghurt, simmer for a moment longer, then cool a little and liquidize.

CURRIED SPINACH SOUP WITH AUBERGINE

With its slightly chewy texture and distinctively smoky taste, aubergine is one of the best meat substitutes in a vegetarian diet. It is also quite difficult to make into satisfactory soups, since it does not respond well to being puréed and diluted with water. In this soup, however, the aubergines remain in cubes or dice, as in ratatouille, and are added in the final stage to give a pleasant contrast to the smoothness of the curried spinach. A gentle soup with only the mildest taste of curry.

2 aubergines
sea salt
2 onions, peeled and chopped
3–4 tablespoons sunflower oil
1 large chilli pepper, de-seeded and
   finely chopped
1 teaspoon each cumin, coriander and
   cardamom seeds

1 thimble-sized piece ginger root,
   peeled
6–8 cloves garlic, peeled
75–110 g/3–4 oz tamarind or
   4–5 tomatoes, skinned and
   chopped
900 g/2 lb spinach
700–850 ml/1¼–1½ pints water
110 g/4 oz Greek strained yoghurt

An hour before cooking the soup, slice the aubergines, sprinkle salt on both sides of the slices and prop them against one another on their edges on a large dinner plate to exude their liquid. (Half an hour will do, if the salting process continues for a further 30 minutes while you carry out the first stages of making the soup.)

Soften the onions in 1 tablespoon of sunflower oil in a heavy, covered pan. After 10 minutes or so add the finely chopped chilli pepper, then the spices, ground together in a mortar, then the ginger root, chopped and crushed with half the garlic cloves and a little sea salt. Add the rest of the garlic cloves, halved, directly to the mixture in the pan. Use tamarind if possible in this soup (soaked and strained as in the previous recipe), since its acidic taste complements that of the aubergine; but, failing that, add the skinned and roughly chopped tomatoes and cook uncovered for 5–10 minutes as if for a sauce. Wash the spinach well and cram it into the pan with 1 teaspoon of sea salt, turn up the heat and cook quite fast for 5–10 minutes until the spinach is bubbling in liquid and has shrunk somewhat in bulk. (If your original pan was too small to contain it all, you could reduce the spinach in a separate pan, then transfer it into the curry sauce.) Top up with 700–850 ml/1¼–1½ pints of water, bring to the boil, simmer for about another 10 minutes, then cool a little, add the yoghurt and liquidize. Meanwhile rinse and dry the aubergine slices, cut them into 2.5 cm/1 in cubes and shallow-fry them in 2–3 tablespoons of sunflower oil until they are brown and crisp on the cut surfaces but not burnt. Add them to the liquidized soup like croûtons, leave it to stand for a little for the flavours to interact, then re-warm it if necessary and serve.

This is not a soup you can keep, although it might be frozen or stored in the refrigerator if the aubergine were omitted until just before serving.

STOCK-BASED
SOUPS

Victorians, who drew fine distinctions between beef consommé, inferior second stock, coarse mutton broth, light veal stock and its alternative, chicken broth, maintaining the stockpot, or a battery of separate stock-pots for different uses, was something of a sacred duty. With our more vegetable-oriented cookery, we can appreciate a vegetable soup without assuming that, if not based on a rich beef stock, it must be based on a pale veal or chicken one. Yet we can also make good stock from the bones of a chicken, duck or pheasant if we happen to have one in the house, and use this for risotto, braised vegetables or any of those soups in which stock is either necessary or a pleasant addition. Chicken stock, so important in both Chinese and East European Jewish cookery, is an excellent back-ground to a mixture of vegetables and to beans or split peas. Unlike beef stock it is also very palatable on its own, or with rice or pasta (*riso in brodo, tortellini in brodo*) as served as a first course at dinner in Italy. In this section I have mainly included recipes calling for chicken or duck stock, with only two which specifically call for beef bone broth or for a stock of oxtail.

Chicken stock can vary in intensity and flavour, depending on whether it is simply made from the chicken bones after they have already been cooked, for example by roasting, or whether it is made by boiling the whole chicken or part of one so that it is flavoured by the flesh as well as the bones. To make a simple chicken stock from bones, put the carcase and any residual skin (but *not* leftover bread sauce or stuffing) into the bottom half of a fairly large saucepan or casserole with a tightly fitting lid. Cover the bones with water, add an onion, a teaspoon of sea salt and half a dozen black peppercorns, bring the water to the boil and simmer it, covered, for 2 to 4 hours. Do not leave the stock on overnight, since, apart from the penetrating smell which results when windows are left closed, an over-cooked stock can taste as bitter as an undercooked one tastes anaemic. A superior stock can be made in just over an hour if you boil a chicken whole with a cut lemon inside it and simmer small whole carrots or cut-up larger ones, onions and celery or leeks in the water with it. Pre-frying chicken bones in butter also adds extra richness to stock. When the stock is cooked, strain it into a basin, cover it and leave it to cool before refrigerating. Several hours in the refrigerator may jellify it or leave it in a liquid state with an easily removable lid of fat. In either case the fat should be easy enough to skim or strain off the top. Use bone stock within 2 or 3 days, re-boiling it daily in hot weather, or freeze it in ice trays after skimming off all fat.

BEEF AND PRUNE SOUP WITH DUMPLINGS

A rich, rewarding soup, well worth the effort of seeking out a butcher who has beef bones to spare. The slightly un-English addition of prunes to the beef broth gives it colour and a memorable flavour, but not too much sweetness.

1 kg / 2½ lb beef bones
275 g / 10 oz lean stewing beef
5–6 black peppercorns
1 bayleaf (optional)
1.75 litres / 3 pints water
1 teaspoon sea salt
1 onion, peeled and chopped
1 carrot, peeled and chopped
1 tablespoon sunflower oil
6–8 medium to large prunes with
   1 cup prune juice

FOR 16–18 LARGE DUMPLINGS
150 g / 5 oz wholemeal flour
50 g / 2 oz suet (I use vegetable suet)
1¼ teaspoons baking powder
⅔ teaspoon sea salt
freshly ground black pepper
6 tablespoons cold water

Six or eight beef bones, each roughly 15 cm/6 in long, should fit comfort-
ably into a 3.5 to 4.5 litre/6 to 8 pint casserole. Tuck a piece of stewing
beef down among them, add 5–6 black peppercorns and a bay-leaf if you
have one, and cover with 1.75 litres/3 pints of water with 1 teaspoon of sea
salt. Bring this to the boil, skim off the first greyish froth, put the lid on
and simmer for 2–2½ hours.

Meanwhile soak and cook the prunes. Put the dry ingredients for the
dumplings in a mixing bowl, rub the suet into the flour, then gradually add
enough cold water to make a consistent dough, cutting it into the flour
and suet with a knife blade until the dough is ready to be taken up and
shaped into a ball by hand. Wrap this in foil and chill it in the refrigerator
for an hour or so.

When the stock is ready, move it to one side and, in a smaller pan,
gently cook together the chopped onion and carrot in 1 tablespoon of sunflower oil for 15 minutes with the lid on. Cook the prunes in just over a
cupful of water in another pan, or use pre-cooked prunes and a cupful of
their juice. Strain the stock, discarding the meat and bones, and pour it
into a tall, narrow jug from which the surface layer of fat may be easily
removed by skimming or blotting it with kitchen paper. By now a certain
amount of the original water will have evaporated, and you should have
1.2–1.5 litres/2–2½ pints of liquid in all.

Shape the dumplings into balls roughly halfway in size between a large
marble and a ping-pong ball, and boil them for about 20 minutes in a
large, covered pan of lightly salted water without removing the lid during
cooking. Meanwhile pour the skimmed beef stock into the pan with the
cooked onion and carrot and add the stoned prunes, their juice and (if
you are as addicted to them as I am) the kernels from the stones. Bring
these to the boil, simmer them together for 15–20 minutes, cool a little
and liquidize. Return the soup to the pan, add the drained dumplings and
serve, allowing at least 3 dumplings to each bowl of soup.

If you prefer, the dumplings may be cooked in the liquidized soup, or
even in the unliquidized soup if you are prepared to remove them and keep
them warm while liquidizing.

NOTE

For a simple family supper, this is lovely on a winter evening with a chopped, raw celery salad and a creamy pudding or large, juicy Moroccan oranges to follow. I suggest a rich, spicy baked custard, which can be mixed in 5 minutes and cooked in just over half an hour. Instead of eggs and milk, use eggs and Greek yoghurt (three small eggs to 400 g/14 oz of yoghurt), blending in 75–110 g/3–4 oz brown sugar, cinnamon, nutmeg, and 150 ml/¼ pint of milk, or 50–75 g/2–3 oz curd or cream cheese for extra richness.

GREEN VELVET (BROAD BEAN TOP) SOUP

Nutty-tasting broad bean tops, with their smooth, spinach-like texture, are unfortunately not a crop which ever find their way into greengrocers' shops in June or July. Nor do gardening books, in their instructions about 'pinching out' bean tops to deter blackfly, ever tell you that the tops are not only edible but delicious. It was therefore years before I discovered how wrong I had been to discard the snipped-off tops on to the compost heap. The late Marika Hanbury-Tenison, in *Cooking with Vegetables* (1980), wrote that she sometimes wondered if she cultivated broad bean plants for the tops more than for the beans themselves. Her recipe, for a solid dish named Materlone, involves minced lamb, onions, bacon and mushroom ketchup. More conventionally, I am happy to eat broad bean tops as a vegetable, plainly boiled like spinach with a little *shoyu* or *tamari,* or in a soup, which conserves their broad-bean flavour while allowing them to be liquidized into complete smoothness.

2 onions, peeled and chopped
2 tablespoons sunflower oil
2 courgettes, sliced
225 g/8 oz broad bean tops
1 teaspoon sea salt

1.5 litres/2½ pints chicken stock,
or 1.2 litres/2 pints water plus
1–2 tablespoons shoyu or tamari
2 handfuls sorrel leaves (optional)

Soften the onions in 2 tablespoons of sunflower oil in a heavy, covered pan. After 10 minutes add the sliced courgettes and cook them for another 5–10 minutes over a low to moderate heat, stirring every now and again to make sure that they do not brown. Wash the bean tops, checking them carefully for signs of blackfly, and add them to the pan. Cover with the stock, add the sea salt if the stock is unsalted, bring to the boil and simmer for 20 minutes before liquidizing. In the absence of stock, use water but season with 1–2 tablespoons of *shoyu* or *tamari* before serving. Just before the end of cooking, add the sorrel if you have some for extra sharpness and smoothness.

A thick, smooth, dark green soup with a subtle and interesting taste.

Fresh White Haricot Bean Soup

A soup for campers in France (hence the stock-cube), although those with a solid roof over their heads can of course make their own chicken stock, improving the quality of this open-air soup.

Fresh *haricots blancs* in withered, papery, sometimes pink- and purple-speckled pods can be found for sale in northern French greengrocers' and supermarkets during the holiday months of high summer. Despite their sometimes bizarre appearance they have a particularly delicate taste in soup.

2 onions	1.5 litres / 2½ pints chicken stock
2 carrots	(stock-cube permitted)
2 tablespoons sunflower oil	sea salt
1 kg / 2¼ lb fresh white haricot beans	

Peel and finely chop the onions and carrots and soften them gently for 10–15 minutes in 2 tablespoons of sunflower oil in a heavy, covered pan. Meanwhile shell the beans and discard the pods. Add the beans and stock or stock-cube and water to the pan, season with sea salt if necessary, bring to the boil and simmer for 20–30 minutes until the beans are soft. Serve out of doors, sitting on the ground, with a rough, red wine, French bread, ham or pâté and a salad.

Minestrone (High Summer Variety)

Recipes for minestrone come with as many variations as there are books in English about Italian food. There are the classic regional variations, with pesto, pumpkin or other special ingredients, and the individual quirks of taste which may or may not include cabbage, carrots, potatoes, red or green peppers, or dried haricot or kidney beans. A basic minestrone, if there is such a thing, must be stock-based; it must include a mixture of root and leaf vegetables, all finely chopped; it must, in addition, include either pasta or dried beans; and it must be served with plenty of freshly grated Parmesan cheese. Within this framework the possible variations are so many that I cannot give a single definitive recipe for minestrone or, indeed, list the variations individually. Unless one is intent on regional authenticity the answer is probably to consider the season of the year, since it is obviously better to use whatever vegetables are fresh than to concoct a supposedly correct soup largely out of frozen ones. As nobody wants dried beans in summer I have treated this summer minestrone principally as a fresh bean soup, with other seasonal vegetables for a harmonious background.

2 onions, peeled and chopped

4 tablespoons olive oil

4 thin leeks, washed

6 sticks celery, washed

2 courgettes, washed

6 cloves garlic, peeled

6 tomatoes, skinned and chopped

1 tablespoon fresh thyme, oregano or
   marjoram

sea salt

freshly ground black pepper

pinch of sugar (optional)

1.75 litres/3 pints chicken stock

110–175 g/4–6 oz shelled broad
   beans

110–175 g/4–6 oz French or
   runner beans, chopped

110–175 g/4–6 oz shelled peas

a handful of small pasta

a few spinach or sorrel leaves

1 tablespoon fresh basil, chopped

Parmesan, to serve

Soften the peeled and chopped onion in 3 tablespoons of olive oil in a large, heavy, covered pan. Add the finely chopped leeks and celery and soften these for another 10 minutes, then stir in the finely diced courgette and continue softening for a further 5–10 minutes. Add half the garlic, cut into slices, then the skinned and roughly chopped tomatoes, the thyme, oregano or marjoram and the rest of the garlic, crushed in a mortar with a little sea salt. Cook uncovered as if for a sauce while the tomatoes disintegrate and become imbued with the flavour of the herbs and garlic. Season with salt, pepper and a little sugar if necessary; add the strained stock, the beans and the peas; bring the soup to the boil and simmer it for about 30 minutes. After 15 minutes add the pasta and the washed and torn-up spinach or sorrel leaves, stirring them well in. Before serving, stir in an extra tablespoon of olive oil and let the soup cool almost to luke-warm to allow the different flavours of the vegetables to emerge. Sprinkle with chopped basil, which loses its flavour in cooking, and serve with good bread and plenty of freshly grated Parmesan.

MINESTRONE (SIMPLE WINTER VARIETY)

Cabbage often features in winter vegetable soups, such as minestrone or the French *garbure*, but I have omitted it from this soup since I prefer to balance cabbage with a strong, single meaty or spicy taste which is not included here. A few florets of cauliflower cut up very small, a fine leek or two, or a few shredded leaves of chard (perpetual spinach) are all acceptable to give extra vegetable interest to this soup.

2 onions, peeled
2 carrots, peeled
2 sticks celery, washed
1 large red pepper, de-seeded
3 tablespoons olive oil
2 courgettes, washed
3 red-skinned potatoes, scrubbed
4 tomatoes, skinned and chopped
4 cloves garlic, peeled
sea salt

1 tablespoon fresh thyme, oregano or marjoram, or frozen basil
freshly ground black pepper
pinch of sugar (optional)
1.5 litres/2½ pints chicken stock
400 g/14 oz cooked dried haricot beans
a few spinach or sorrel leaves
Parmesan, to serve

Soften the finely chopped onions, carrots, celery and pepper in 3 table-spoons of olive oil. After 10–15 minutes stir in the finely diced courgettes and potatoes and soften for another 5 minutes, then add the tomatoes, the crushed garlic and the herbs. Cook uncovered over a raised heat as if for a sauce for 5–10 minutes, seasoning with salt, pepper and a little sugar if necessary. Then pour on the stock, bring it to the boil, add the drained, cooked beans and simmer for 30 minutes until the beans are disintegrating gently into the liquid. Add the washed and torn spinach or sorrel leaves just before the end and allow them to turn limp and almost black, but allow 5 minutes longer for chard and make sure that the thick stems have been discarded. Cool the soup slightly and serve with plenty of freshly grated Parmesan.

CABBAGE AND HOT PEPPER SOUP

As with minestrone, there are many versions of cabbage and red pepper soup. One of the most popular is *Mayorquina*, described by Elizabeth David (*French Country Cooking*, 1966). This version substitutes potatoes for leeks, since there is something particularly exciting in the combination of peppers and potatoes, which is perhaps traceable to their shared member-ship of the *Solanaceae* family. The chilli pepper gives a faintly Hungarian taste to the soup, and needs the bland richness of chicken stock to counter-balance its fierceness.

This soup is not liquidized, so all the vegetables should be chopped quite finely.

2 large onions, peeled and chopped

3–4 tablespoons olive oil

2 large peppers, de-seeded, or
    1 400 g / 14 oz tin pepper salad

1 large chilli pepper, de-seeded

700 g / 1½ lb firm, white cabbage

2 potatoes, unpeeled

450 g / 1 lb tomatoes, skinned and
    chopped

6–8 large cloves garlic, peeled

1.5 litres / 2½ pints chicken stock

1 teaspoon sea salt

slices of wholemeal bread

Parmesan cheese

Soften the onions in 2 tablespoons of olive oil in a heavy, covered pan. After 5–10 minutes add the chopped peppers and the whole or halved, chilli pepper. If using tinned pepper salad instead of fresh peppers, add this later on with the tomatoes. Then stir in the finely shredded cabbage, minus the stalk and any tough outer leaves, and the scrubbed, unpeeled and diced potatoes. Cook the vegetables for a minute or two longer in their own steam, removing the lid every now and then to stir them since cabbage burns easily, and adding another 1–2 tablespoons of oil. Add the tomatoes and half the cloves of garlic, crushed, slicing the others straight into the pan, and cook uncovered for 5–10 minutes over a moderate heat while seasoning and breaking up the tomatoes. If you have no red peppers, a 400 g / 14 oz tin of pepper salad may be added at this stage. Pour on the strained and skimmed stock, bring to the boil and simmer for 20–30 minutes. Add a teaspoon of sea salt if the stock has not previously been seasoned. Before serving, remove the chilli pepper and pour the soup over slices of home-made wholemeal bread placed in individual bowls. Sprinkle generously with freshly grated Parmesan cheese.

CARROT, CHICKEN AND SPINACH SOUP

A good soup for a cold, bracing winter lunchtime when you happen to have chicken stock to hand but have a limited choice of vegetables. The richer the stock, the better it will bring out the golden warmth of the carrots. If using duck stock instead, or a stock made with a mixture of chicken and duck bones, so much the better.

2 onions
2 tablespoons olive oil
4 cloves garlic, peeled
450 g / 1 lb carrots, peeled and
   chopped
15 g / ½ oz butter
sea salt

6 green peppercorns
½ teaspoon brown sugar
½ teaspoon freshly grated nutmeg
1.2 litres / 2 pints good chicken stock
225 g / 8 oz summer spinach or
   1 oz fresh parsley, washed

Peel and chop the onions and soften them in 2 tablespoons of olive oil in a heavy, covered pan. After 5–10 minutes add the halved garlic cloves, then the roughly chopped carrots with the butter. Stir gently and continue softening with the lid on for another 15 minutes until the carrots, onions and garlic are bubbling in a buttery juice. Add a large pinch of sea salt (or 1 teaspoon if the stock is unsalted), half a dozen green peppercorns and half a teaspoon each of brown sugar and freshly grated nutmeg. Stir well together, then pour on the stock, bring to the boil and simmer for 20–30 minutes. Towards the end of the cooking time, add the spinach leaves or the de-stalked and chopped parsley. Cool a little and liquidize.

A sweet and savoury soup with a nice, fresh green touch which cuts through the richness of the butter and stock.

Spinach Soup with Yellow Beans and Wok-fried Vegetables

For an instant Chinese taste, a tin of yellow beans in salted sauce can be excellent value. These fermented soya beans in their pungent sauce can be overpowering if eaten plain with rice or bean curd; but they do wonders in spicing up a plain, velvety spinach soup. For sweetness and contrast in texture, the added matchstick carrots are essential. Serve the soup with red-cooked bean curd (*tofu*) and fried or sizzling rice for a complete, satisfying meal.

2 onions, peeled and chopped	700–850 ml / 1¼–1½ pints chicken
2–4 tablespoons sunflower oil	stock
3–4 cloves garlic, peeled and chopped	sea salt
450 g / 1 lb summer spinach, washed	2 large carrots
2 tablespoons yellow beans in salted	110 g / 4 oz mushrooms
sauce	10 g / ¼ oz ginger root
8 green peppercorns	

Soften the onions in 2 tablespoons of sunflower oil in a deep, heavy, covered pan. Add the chopped cloves of garlic, then the spinach and the yellow beans. Do not add salt at this stage. Leave the spinach to cook for 5 minutes without adding any liquid, then strain on the stock, add the peppercorns, bring to the boil and simmer for 15–20 minutes. Taste for seasoning and add salt if necessary.

To finish the soup, which at this stage will be pungent but slightly bitter, you will need a wok to stir-fry the remaining vegetables to the right degree of chewy sweetness. Peel the carrots and cut them into matchstick-lengths. (Parsnips, or a mixture of parsnip and carrot, would do just as well.) Wash or wipe the mushrooms and slice them thinly. Heat a little oil in the wok; peel the slice of ginger root and smash it with a wooden spoon or pestle to break up the fibres while keeping it whole; then stir-fry the carrots with the ginger for 1–2 minutes until they have turned pale and begun to brown at the edges. Discard the ginger, add the drained carrots to the soup, then lightly fry the mushroom slices and add them also to the soup.

COLD CHICKEN, CELERY AND WALNUT SOUP

Nut soups are not to everybody's taste; but this is quite an elegant one, reminiscent of a very liquid *hummus*, and it is best eaten cold, as a good background to a simple supper of brown rice and vegetables, perhaps with an additional dish of prawns.

2 chicken legs	2 heads celery, washed
2 onions, peeled	2–3 tablespoons olive oil
1 carrot, peeled	5–6 cloves garlic, peeled
6 black peppercorns	200–225 g/7–8 oz shelled walnuts
sea salt	2 tablespoons Greek strained yoghurt
1.5 litres/2½ pints water	freshly ground black pepper

Remove all skin and fat from the chicken legs, place them in a saucepan with one of the onions, the carrot, half a dozen black peppercorns and a large pinch of sea salt, cover with the water, bring to the boil and simmer for 40–45 minutes. Halfway through this time, chop up the remaining onion and the celery and put them to soften in the olive oil in a heavy, covered pan. When they are soft and the chicken is cooked through, strain nearly all the stock from round the chicken over the onion and celery and continue simmering for another 15–20 minutes. Strip the chicken meat from the bones and cover it with the remaining spoonful or so of stock to keep it moist. Discard the bones and the carrot and onion from the stock.

In a large mortar or small pudding basin, crush the garlic with a little sea salt. Pound the walnuts into this until they are quite fine (or, if you like, crush them in an electric blender first; but do not add the garlic, as the blender would have a brutalizing effect on its eventual taste). Then pound in the chicken meat, which should be quite soft. Bind this mixture with the yoghurt, season it with freshly ground black pepper, liquidize the celery soup and stir the chicken and nut mixture in. Chill before eating.

The soup may be put through a *moulin-légumes* for a smoother texture.

CELERY AND DUCK SOUP WITH DUCK AND WALNUT PÂTÉ

If you decide to make both soup and pâté, this will require a whole duck and the pâté will need to be made the day before the soup in order to free the bones for making stock. Otherwise, you can simply make the soup with the carcase of a roast duck and omit the pâté altogether. Celery is one of the best possible accompaniments to a roast duck, either in this soup or braised in the liquid in which the duck has been cooked and then dried out a little in a covered dish in the oven.

FOR THE STOCK
1 duck carcase
2.25 litres/4 pints water
1 onion, peeled
1 teaspoon sea salt
black peppercorns

FOR THE SOUP
2 large onions, peeled and chopped
2 carrots, peeled and chopped
2 tablespoons olive oil
1 large or 2 medium heads celery
1.75 litres/3 pints duck stock (see below)
sea salt
freshly ground black pepper

Make the stock a day before the soup, either by pot-roasting the duck to make pâté as described in the following recipe, or by simply covering the duck bones with water, adding a peeled onion, 1 teaspoon of sea salt and a few black peppercorns and simmering, covered, for 2–4 hours. Strain and cool the stock, refrigerate it overnight and remove the layer of fat next day.

Soften the chopped onions and carrots in the oil in a heavy, covered pan. Wash, scrape and chop up the celery and stir it in. Continue cooking for 15–20 minutes in the steam produced by the celery. Pour on the stock, bring it to the boil and simmer for 20–30 minutes. Cool a little, add salt if necessary and a little freshly ground black pepper and liquidize.

A frothy, rich, light soup.

DUCK AND WALNUT PÂTÉ

Elizabeth David, in *Spices, Salt and Aromatics in the English Kitchen* (1970), gives a very similar recipe to this under the name of *fezanjan*. It originated, she tells us, in the British Embassy in Teheran; and her source for it was Sir Harry Luke's *The Tenth Muse* (1954). Our Iranian lodger acknowledged the existence of a dish named *fezanjan* but refused to recognize any connection between it and the dish which I served her. It is, nevertheless, very good, and she ate it with every appearance of enjoyment.

1 medium-sized (1 kg/2½ lb)
   roasting duck
2 tablespoons olive oil
275 ml/½ pint water
6–8 sticks celery (optional)

110–150 g/4–5 oz shelled walnuts
10–12 allspice berries
3–4 tablespoons shoyu or tamari
juice of 1 grapefruit

Find a heavy casserole into which the duck will fit. Failing that, cut off the rear end of the carcase behind the legs and cook it separately for stock. Fry the duck on all sides in hot olive oil until the skin is crisp, then pour in the water, put the lid on and simmer the duck over a low heat for about 1½ hours. For the last 30 minutes you could slip in some sticks of celery to braise in the thick, juicy liquid surrounding the duck.

Pound the walnuts and allspice together to a paste in a large mortar or small pudding basin, then remove the duck from its liquid, pour off as much as you can of the surface fat without wasting the meaty juices underneath, and mix the rest of the juices with the walnuts and allspice. Add the *shoyu* or *tamari* and grapefruit juice to taste. (The British Embassy recipe stipulated gravy browning and pomegranate juice, in the best tradition of mixing home comforts with exotic native specialities.) Keep the sauce warming gently in a small casserole while you strip the meat from the duck, which is best kept warm on a dish in a low oven while you remove small portions of it one at a time. Piece by piece, take legs and slices of breast from the warming-dish, cut them up small and add them to the sauce, while keeping the bones for stock. When you have finished, cover the casserole and gently cook the meat in the sauce for another 15–20 minutes, then either serve it warm with brown rice and a salad or leave it to cool and solidify.

If making soup, cover the bones and any unused pieces of duck meat with 1.75 litres/3 pints of water, add 1 peeled onion, 1 teaspoon of sea salt and a few black peppercorns, bring to the boil and simmer for 2–4 hours. Refrigerate both stock and pâté overnight. The following day, remove any surface pools of fat from the pâté and turn it out on to a small dish to serve.

Apricot, Duck and Orange Soup with Watercress

If you have a liking for quite sweet soups, this one is worth trying when you have spare duck stock. It is very good for an informal supper at which the soup can be eaten with, rather than before, a number of other dishes: for example, a big dish of brown rice or a brown rice salad containing mushrooms, nuts and diced red peppers; a duck or chicken mayonnaise; and a red or green salad of radicchio or watercress and oak-leaf lettuce.

2 onions, peeled and chopped
2 carrots, peeled and chopped
2 tablespoons sunflower oil
2 large cloves garlic
1 thimble-sized piece ginger root
sea salt
225 g / 8 oz dried apricots

1.75 litres / 3 pints duck stock
freshly ground black pepper
2 tablespoons shoyu or tamari
juice of 2 oranges
2 bunches watercress, cleaned and
    chopped

Soften the onions and carrots in 2 tablespoons of sunflower oil in a heavy, covered pan. Peel and cut up the garlic and ginger, crush them together with a little sea salt and add them to the onions and carrots. Wash the apricots thoroughly, getting rid of all pockets of grit, and add them to the pan with the well-skimmed stock. Bring this to the boil and simmer it for 30 minutes, during which time the apricots will soften and expand. Season with 1 good teaspoon of sea salt and some freshly ground black pepper and liquidize. Add *shoyu* or *tamari* and orange juice to taste, and serve garnished with plenty of watercress, which makes a good contrast in both colour and flavour with this thick, sweetish, orange soup.

DUCK SOUP WITH WOK-FRIED JULIENNE VEGETABLES

This fresh-tasting soup is the perfect lunchtime by-product of a more substantial supper dish involving poaching a whole duck in liquid, then using only part of the stock. Sainsburys now sell Barbary ducks which, being lean, are well suited to this kind of treatment. Below I give my recipe for duck with potatoes in a ginger-flavoured broth, from which the rich stock needed as the basis for this soup may be derived.

FOR THE STOCK
1 medium-sized duck (1–1.35 kg/
   2½–3 lb), de-fatted and skinned
2 teaspoons dried lemon grass
6–8 green peppercorns
2.25 litres/4 pints water

FOR THE SOUP
2–3 parsnips
2–3 carrots
175 g/6 oz dwarf French beans
3–4 spring onions
1.2 litres/2 pints duck stock
1 tablespoon sunflower oil
sea salt
freshly ground black pepper

Make the stock with the whole fresh duck and the water flavoured with lemon grass and the black peppercorns, simmer for 1 hour, then skim and refrigerate. Peel the parsnips and carrots and cut them into julienne strips. Top-and-tail the beans and spring onions and cut up both into short lengths of 1 cm/½ in or less. Bring the stock to the boil and simmer it gently. In a wok, heat the oil to smoking point and quickly stir-fry the carrots, parsnips and spring onions for a minute or two until they are lightly browned at the edges and sweet-tasting. Add these to the stock with the cut-up beans, bring it back to simmering point and continue cooking for another 10–15 minutes before serving. Season with sea salt and pepper as required.

It is the richness and purity of the strong, dark-coloured duck stock which gives this soup its character and allows the julienne of vegetables to be so simple. Cooking duck itself may alarm some people because of the problem of disposing of the copious fat; but this is not a problem at all if the duck has previously been skinned and de-fatted, and is poached in liquid rather than sautéd or roasted. The following is a main course for 4, using half the stock produced in the process.

Duck and Potatoes in a Ginger-flavoured Broth

1 Barbary duck, 1–1.35 kg/
  2½–3 lb
2.25 litres/4 pints water
6–8 green peppercorns
2 teaspoons dried lemon grass

450 g/1 lb waxy new potatoes
15 g/½ oz ginger root, peeled
2–3 large cloves garlic, peeled
2 tablespoons shoyu or tamari
freshly ground black pepper

Place the skinned and de-fatted duck in a large saucepan and cover it with the water. Add the green peppercorns and the lemon grass, bring the water to the boil and simmer it, covered, for 45 minutes to 1 hour. Wash the potatoes and cut them into slices ½ cm/¼ in thick. Remove the duck to a pre-warmed oven-proof dish and parboil the potatoes briefly in the stock. Strip as much of the duck meat as you intend to use into the dish, and mix into it the crushed ginger root and garlic and the *shoyu* or *tamari*. Arrange the potato slices on top, strain on 570 ml/1 pint or more of the stock, pepper well and bake in a gentle oven, 150–170°C, 300–325°F, gas mark 2–3, for another 30 minutes or so. Serve with broccoli or mangetout peas.

Chestnut and Oxtail Soup

A rich and nourishing soup, which can also be made in half quantities for 2 or 3 people if you simply want to use up the narrow end of an oxtail while stewing the more substantial pieces with vegetables and/or dumplings. Chestnuts are in season from mid-October until just before Christmas, so the day to choose for this is a foggy, cold November one when winter appetites are prepared for gelatinous oxtail meat and its thick, rich gravy. In this soup, both the chestnuts and the carrots add sweetness and counteract any fattiness in the oxtail while preventing the soup from being too predominantly meaty.

450 g / 1 lb chestnuts

2 onions, peeled and chopped

3–4 carrots, peeled and chopped

2 tablespoons olive oil

1 oxtail

a little flour, for coating

1–2 tablespoons sunflower oil

1.5 litres / 2½ pints water

1–2 teaspoons sea salt

freshly ground pepper

Skin the chestnuts by nicking each one on both sides with the point of a sharp knife and placing them under a hot grill for about 5 minutes a side until the hard outer and papery inner skins come away on the point of the knife. Meanwhile soften the onions and carrots in 2 tablespoons of olive oil for 10–15 minutes in a heavy, covered pan. Flour the pieces of oxtail, brown them in a little hot sunflower oil in a frying-pan, then add them, with the skinned chestnuts, to the onions and carrots. Cover with the water, season with sea salt and a little black pepper, bring to the boil and simmer for 40–45 minutes. Remove the oxtail bones, detach any meat that you wish to and add it to the soup, either before or after liquidizing.

A good Sunday lunch soup, qualifying as a meal in itself if eaten with the right kind of bread, and followed perhaps by a choice of different cheeses and an apple tart or a late autumnal quince and ginger cream.

JUNE SOUP

This is really a late spring soup, for that time when nothing yet seems to be properly in season and when cold winds blight the beginning of summer and give one unseasonable longings for warm, comforting soups. This is the time to forget asparagus and turn back to root vegetables, such as the new, sharp-tasting young turnips in their delicately purple-flushed white skins. These go well with the winter and spring perennial, the bulbous Florentine fennel with its faintly aniseed-like taste. The rich, lemony stock, the sharp sorrel and garlicky tomato provide a good background for the pungency of the young turnips and fennel. It is worth boiling a chicken with a cut lemon inside it to produce the right rich, strong broth to pull this soup together, remembering that it is easily a meal in itself.

FOR THE STOCK
1 lemon
1 1.35 kg/3 lb chicken
1 onion, peeled
1 carrot, peeled
6 black peppercorns
1 teaspoon sea salt
1.75 litres/3 pints water

FOR THE SOUP
350 g/12 oz green or yellow split peas
3 onions
6 small, new turnips
3 carrots
3 heads fennel
3–4 tablespoons olive oil
6 cloves garlic, peeled
sea salt
1 400 g/14 oz tin tomatoes
1 tablespoon fresh thyme or marjoram
1.5 litres/2½ pints good chicken stock
*a handful of sorrel or several large
    spinach leaves*

The day before making this soup, place a cut-up lemon inside your chicken and boil for just over 1 hour (for a 1.35 kg/3 pounder), adding a peeled onion and carrot, 6 black peppercorns and 1 good teaspoon of sea salt to the water. Strain off the broth and refrigerate it overnight.

Soak the split peas either overnight or for several hours, then boil them in plenty of unsalted water for 30 minutes to 1 hour until they are soft. The first 10 minutes of boiling should always be fast and uncovered; the rest may be a steady simmer with the lid on. Meanwhile, peel the onions and turnips, and scrape the carrots and fennel; chop them all into small dice and soften them for 15 minutes in 3–4 tablespoons of olive oil in a heavy, covered pan. Crush the garlic in a mortar with a little sea salt and add it to the vegetables with the tomatoes and the thyme or marjoram, raising the heat a little and cooking uncovered for 5–10 minutes while breaking up the tomatoes with a wooden spoon. Then add the drained split peas, the skimmed stock and the washed and torn-up sorrel leaves. (Spinach will do, but it will not contribute such an interestingly acidic flavour.) Bring to the boil, simmer for 30 minutes, cool and serve. Add more salt if the split peas seem to demand it, but do not liquidize the soup unless you want their taste to be dominant.

DECEMBER SOUP

A winter version of June Soup, equally good but slightly sweeter and less acidic. Although I first made it in December, it can in fact be made at any time when parsnips are available, from autumn into spring.

A good, rich stock for this cheerful soup can be made with leftover pieces of uncooked chicken (wings, back, skin) if you have bought a roasting chicken to make one of those dishes in which not all the chicken is used, but for which it is wholly or partially boned and cut up into pieces before cooking. A large-scale purchase of red peppers, for example, could give you casseroled chicken and peppers one night and this soup the next.

350 g / 12 oz yellow split peas

2 onions

3 tablespoons olive oil

2 parsnips, peeled

2 red peppers, de-seeded

6–8 sticks celery, washed

225 g / 8 oz chopped tomatoes

6 cloves garlic, peeled

1–2 teaspoons sea salt

1.5 litres / 2½ pints chicken stock

Soak the split peas overnight or for several hours during the daytime. Cover them with water, boil them hard with the lid off the pan for 10 minutes, then simmer them, covered, for 30 minutes to 1 hour until they are soft. Peel and chop the onions and soften them in 3 tablespoons of olive oil in a heavy, covered pan, adding the finely chopped parsnips, the peppers and the celery, both of which should, again, be cut up fairly finely. When the vegetables have softened, stir in the chopped tomatoes and the chopped or crushed garlic and cook for a little longer until the vegetables are coated in a pungent tomato sauce. Add the drained split peas with 1–2 teaspoons of sea salt (exactly how much will depend on the saltiness or otherwise of the stock), then cover with stock, bring to the boil and simmer for another 15–20 minutes until the split peas have merged with everything else.

Serve with wholemeal or granary bread and grated Parmesan cheese for a nourishing meal.

LEEK AND CHICKEN SOUP

The simplest variation on the classic cock-a-leekie. The soft subtlety of cooked leek combines well with the delicacy of chicken stock, however unsuitable leeks may be as a vegetable dish to serve with chicken.

900 g/2 lb leeks
1.2–1.5 litres/2–2½ pints chicken
    stock, made using 1 leek (see
    below)

2–3 tablespoons olive oil
freshly ground black pepper or whole
    black peppercorns

The day before making this soup, convert the bones of a chicken into stock in which you have included at least one leek. A large, fat one will give plenty of flavour. Strain the stock, discard the bones and the cooked leek, cool and refrigerate the stock and skim off the fat the next day.

Wash the remaining leeks very thoroughly, cutting two lengthways slits in each one to release trapped pockets of grit, and discard the base and the coarsest, muddiest parts of each. Do not, however, throw away all the green part, as this contains the best of the flavour. Cut the leeks into 2.5 cm/1 in long pieces and soften these for 10–15 minutes in 2–3 tablespoons of olive oil in a heavy, covered pan, stirring occasionally to make sure that they are not browning. Pour on the stock, bring to the boil and simmer for another 20–30 minutes, then liquidize. Season with plenty of freshly ground black pepper, or with whole peppercorns crushed coarsely in a mortar and added to the simmering stock.

FRENCH ONION SOUP

I have a sentimental fondness for French onion soup. When I began life alone in a bed-sittingroom with what were optimistically known as 'cooking facilities' (a two-ring cooker, a curtained recess for plates and stores and a share in a nearby bath for washing-up), this was one of the few things that I learnt to cook. In those days I used a beef stock-cube, since the lack of an oven deprived me of such things as chicken carcases, and the taste did not seem so aggressively artificial as it might today. Less so, anyway, than that of the horrible, 'home-made' French onion soup which I have experienced in a roadside country pub, with a thick lid of microwaved, processed cheese concealing a mass of freeze-dried onion particles, caramel colouring, cornflour, monosodium glutamate and boiling water. Real French onion soup is one of the mildest and most soothing dishes, and does not need the layer of cheese which, if misapplied, can turn an ordinary synthetic concoction into an indigestible horror.

900 g/2 lb large, mild onions
25 g/1 oz butter
1–2 tablespoons sunflower oil
1.5–1.75 litres/2½–3 pints chicken
    stock

sea salt
2 tablespoons shoyu or tamari
    (optional)
1 teaspoon Marmite (optional)

Skin the onions and slice them into almost paper-thin rings. Heat the butter and sunflower oil in a large, heavy pan, stir in the onion rings, cover them and cook them over a medium to low heat for 20–30 minutes, stirring them every now and then to make sure that they do not blacken. If experienced at cooking onions, you may do this a little faster; and the oil, in this case, helps to prevent the butter from turning brown. Eventually the onions should be caramelized with a tendency to stick together. Pour on the stock, bring it to the boil and simmer it, covered, for another 15–20 minutes, until the surface is richly flecked with butter and oil. Season with salt and (if you wish) *shoyu* or *tamari* (or a teaspoon of Marmite if you insist on a dark brown colour). The important thing about this soup, however, is the mild sweetness of the stewed onion rings.

Garlic croutons go well with it (see page 31); toasted cheese rather less so.

Parsnip, Chicken and Orange Soup

My family is very fond of roast parsnips with chicken; a fondness which resulted in the discovery of this soup. Like garlic, parsnips give off their full sweetness only when roasted and can taste overbearingly rank when cooked in other ways. Peeled, cut into strips and placed under or next to a chicken, they absorb its juices and emerge stickily crisp yet melting into their accompaniments such as roast potatoes and roast garlic. If roasted with beef they will probably need parboiling for a minute or two if they are not to become too brown and dry.

To make this soup, you will need to use the bones of a previously roasted chicken for the stock; so the best way to do it is to pre-roast some extra parsnips with the chicken and forbear (if you can) from eating them when the roast is hot. Not all the parsnips need to be pre-roasted, but those which are will be sweetly flavoured and nicely imbued with the chicken juices.

Because this soup needs to be quite rich, you can make the stock immediately before the soup itself, provided that you discard the skin of the chicken and any lurking pockets of fatty meat first. Strip the bones, leaving a little lean meat on them to improve the flavour of the stock, and fry them for a few minutes in 15 g/½ oz of butter in a heavy, covered pan, shaking it every now and then to make sure that they do not stick. Cover the bones with 2 litres/3½ pints of water, add 1 teaspoon of salt and half a dozen black peppercorns, bring to the boil and simmer for about 2 hours.

2 onions

3 tablespoons olive oil

10–12 cloves garlic

7–8 parsnips, either fresh or
    pre-roasted

1.75 litres/3 pints good chicken stock

1 teaspoon sea salt

freshly ground black pepper

juice of 1–2 oranges

Peel and chop the onions and soften them in 3 tablespoons of olive oil in a heavy, covered pan. After 10 minutes add the peeled and halved garlic cloves, then the peeled and sliced parsnips, reserving any which have already been roasted to add later. Cook all the vegetables together for 10–15 minutes until they are soft, stirring them occasionally and adding any pre-roasted parsnips a few minutes before the end. The natural sympathy between garlic and parsnips, which is always apparent when they are roasted together with meat, emerges from this preliminary softening process. Strain the hot stock into the vegetable mixture, add the sea salt and some freshly ground black pepper, simmer for 15–20 minutes, then liquidize. Taste for seasoning and add the juice of a freshly squeezed orange, then the juice of another if the taste seems to demand it. The fresh, tart orange juice has a wonderfully civilizing effect on both the parsnips and the rich chicken stock, making this a subtle soup with a refreshing aftertaste.

TOMATO, PARSLEY AND CHICKEN SOUP

Despite temptations to think of parsley as a mere decorative garnish, like those plastic sprigs of the herb which one sees in butchers' shops, this lovely, kitchen-garden soup cannot exist without it. Indeed, parsley grown in the right way is as potent a herb as oregano or basil. Forget the isolated sprigs, or the glass jars of hay-smelling, dried stuff, and think of large, deep-green bunches of the kind that one can buy in good vegetable shops throughout the summer. Parsley at its strongest has an elusive, haunting smell (think of it long-stemmed, along the paths of a vegetable garden in June rain), and can impose its taste on a soup or sauce if chosen well to combine with the other ingredients. I first made this soup for a summer lunch at my sister's house, where her kitchen garden on a Devon hillside burgeons with parsley, and have become a keen buyer of parsley for soup ever since.

It's best made with a rich chicken stock. (I originally used the back and wings of a chicken from which I had previously sliced off the breast- and leg-meat for a supper dish.) When the stock is cold, skim or drain it to remove the fat.

*2 onions or 4 shallots, peeled and
    chopped*
2 tablespoons olive oil
8–10 cloves garlic
*900 g/2 lb tomatoes or 4 large beef
    tomatoes, skinned and chopped*

1 teaspoon sugar
½ teaspoon salt
freshly ground black pepper
50 g/2 oz parsley, chopped
1.2 litres/2 pints rich chicken stock

Soften the onions or shallots in 2 tablespoons of olive oil in a heavy, covered pan. Add the peeled and chopped garlic cloves, then the tomatoes, season with the sugar, sea salt and freshly ground black pepper, and cook uncovered for 10–15 minutes as if for a sauce. When this has thickened, stir in the chopped parsley and pour on the stock. Bring to the boil, simmer for 10–15 minutes, cool a little and liquidize.

FISH
AND
SEAFOOD
SOUPS

Despite the popular historical depiction of the British as a sea-girt, island race, we have always been inclined, unless we live there, to regard the sea-side as a foreign country, and to look on fish as an exotic and often suspect form of food. Compare, for example, the gastronomic offerings of Dieppe or Le Havre with those of Newhaven or Southampton, and the almost fishless basis of our culture is immediately apparent. London, with its whelks and cockles, its oysters, sole and turbot, was once famous for fish; but the disappearance of fish shops and markets from the centre has long since put an end to the sight of middle-aged businessmen picking up fresh fish for the family's supper. As for fish soup, this has never caught on to the extent that it has in the Channel or Mediterranean ports of France. To the conventional, old-fashioned Englishman, soup and fish were two quite separate, successive courses in the same meal and fish soup virtually a con-tradiction in terms. Hence, perhaps, the rapturous sense of discovery with which adventurous travellers described dishes such as *bouillabaisse*. Our most usual fish (mackerel, herrings, pilchards, plaice, cod) do not seem to lend themselves well to soup-making, either because they are too oily or because they do not have enough bones to make good stock; and we are not used to mixing different kinds of fish together, or fish with molluscs and other seafood, to make a characterful, fresh-tasting fish soup.

This section, therefore, is something of an afterthought. I make no attempt to include in it any of the classic fish soups which can be eaten in French restaurants and are described in books about French cooking, since these can be difficult (and expensive) to make with the material available from the average inland English fish shop. Instead I have slanted it heavily in favour of cheap, reliable and relatively tasty seafood such as prawns and mussels, and have made much use of salmon-heads, which are well-flavoured, cheap and fairly widely available.

MUSSEL SOUP

Another favourite of recent cookery writers. The two great virtues of mussels, which count in their favour against the fears of allergic reactions which they sometimes inspire, are their cheapness and their abundant, tasty juice. We have already met them in combination with avocado pears; but they go equally well in soup with red peppers, spinach and tomatoes. In this soup the taste of the mussels themselves predominates, with an incidental seasoning of garlic, parsley and lemon juice.

900 g/2 lb mussels
2 onions, peeled and chopped
2 tablespoons olive oil
4 cloves garlic, peeled
50 g/2 oz butter

50 g/2 oz flour
850 ml/1½ pints water
4 tablespoons chopped parsley
juice of 2 lemons
1 teaspoon sea salt

Scrub the mussels, rinsing them well and tugging off the 'beard' from each, and throw away any which have damaged shells or are already open. Put the mussels in a heavy, covered pan and cook them over a gentle heat for 15 minutes until they have opened and are swimming in their own bubbling juices. Throw away any which refuse to open after 15–20 minutes' cooking.

Meanwhile, soften the onions in 2 tablespoons of olive oil in another pan. After 10 minutes add the halved garlic cloves and allow them to soften for a few minutes longer. Melt in the butter, stir in the flour, cook it for a few minutes, then gradually stir in the mussel juices. When they have been absorbed, continue thinning with 850 ml/1½ pints of water, bring it to just below the boil and simmer it very gently for 5–10 minutes, adding the parsley, the lemon juice and sea salt. Shell the mussels into the soup, discarding the shells, and liquidize it immediately. This counteracts much of the squeamishness which some people may feel about the texture of mussels. You may of course, however, leave all or some of them whole.

RED PEPPER SOUP WITH MUSSELS

A brilliantly red, rich-tasting soup.

900 g/2 lb mussels
4 large red peppers, de-seeded
12 medium to large cloves garlic,
  peeled

2 tablespoons olive oil
850 ml/1½ pints water
1 teaspoon sea salt

Clean the mussels and put them in a cast-iron casserole to stew, covered, in their own juices for 15 minutes. In another pan, soften the chopped peppers and the sliced garlic cloves in 2 tablespoons of olive oil, stirring them occasionally to make sure that they do not brown. After 10–15 minutes pour on the mussel juices and simmer the peppers and garlic in them for about another 15 minutes, adding 850 ml/1½ pints of water and 1 teaspoon of sea salt as soon as the peppers and garlic have begun to absorb the mussel juices. Keep the mussels warm in their shells by leaving the lid firmly on the casserole in which they were cooked. Liquidize the soup, either before or after you shell the mussels into it, or eat them separately if you prefer.

THICK GREEN MUSSEL SOUP

This more elaborate recipe makes a slightly larger quantity of soup than the two previous mussel-soup recipes: enough for 6–8 rather than enough for

4–6, as the first course of a fairly substantial meal. It's ideal followed by a simple but filling cheese dish such as a leek or aubergine *gougère* which takes 45 minutes to bake and so can be left in the oven to cook while you assemble your soup.

900 g/2 lb mussels	*900 g/2 lb spinach*
2 onions, peeled and chopped	*sea salt*
3 tablespoons olive oil	*4 large cloves garlic, peeled*
450 g/1 lb mushrooms, cleaned	*1.2–1.5 litres/2–2½ pints water*

Clean the mussels and put them to cook gently for 15 minutes in a heavy, covered pan until they are awash with foaming juice. Meanwhile soften the onions in 3 tablespoons of olive oil in another pan, stirring in the roughly sliced mushrooms after about 15 minutes. Wash the spinach in 2 or 3 changes of water and put it in a third, large pan with a little sea salt and no water except what is on the leaves when the spinach is lifted straight into the pan at the end of the last rinse. Boil the spinach hard with the lid on for 5–10 minutes, drain it and discard the water unless you enjoy its slight roughness. Nutritionally it has little to offer, so do not include it in the soup as a pious exercise in vitamin-conservation, and still less as a means of increasing your intake of iron. Chop the spinach roughly and add it to the onions and mushrooms, which should by now be immersed in blackish mushroom juice. Crush the garlic with a little sea salt and stir it in, then add the mussel juice and the water. Bring this to the boil and simmer it gently for 10–15 minutes. Shell in the mussels while the soup is simmering, remove it from the heat and liquidize.

LEEK AND PRAWN SOUP WITH BEAN CURD (TOFU)

Leeks go well in Chinese-tasting dishes such as a stir-fry, on which this surprisingly sustaining soup is based. As a widespread vegetable throughout the ancient world, leeks may have been eaten since time immemorial in China, where their affinity with bean curd is recognized in traditional stir-fry dishes. (See, for example, Buwei Yang Chao, *How to Cook and Eat in Chinese*, 1962.) Now almost reinvented by commercial purveyors of health food, soya bean curd or *tofu* is available in most health-food shops in a variety of pre-packaged consistencies. Twenty years ago, when I shopped at Ceres in the Portobello Road on my way home from work, bean curd was a rarity, in fluctuating supply, sold by the 110 g/¼ lb from a plastic washing-up bowl in which it must have been delivered by an oriental food supplier. Now it comes in 285 g/10½ oz packets, with suggestions for 'Tofu Burgers/Chilli con Tofu/Curried Tofu/Tofu Banana Whip . . .' The kind to look for is Original Tofu, the solider version.

---

700 g/1½ lb prawns in their shells
1.75 litres/3 pints water
sea salt
700 g/1½ lb small, delicate leeks

450 g/1 lb solid bean curd (tofu)
6–8 cloves garlic, peeled
15 g/½ oz slice ginger root
2 tablespoons sunflower oil

Shell the prawns, put the shells and heads in a saucepan with 1.75 litres/ 3 pints of water and a little sea salt, cover and simmer for 30 minutes to make stock. Wash the leeks and slice them finely. Cut the drained *tofu* into 1 cm/½ in squares. Crush the garlic cloves with a little sea salt. Peel the slice of ginger and half crush it to release the juice from the fibres. When the stock is done, stir-fry the *tofu* with the ginger in 2 tablespoons of sunflower oil in a large heavy pan or wok until it is crisp and golden. Set it on one side to keep warm and stir-fry the leeks for a few minutes with the ginger and the garlic. Discard the ginger, pour the strained stock over the leeks and *tofu* and simmer gently together for a few minutes, then add the prawns and serve at once, or keep back half the prawns to serve separately as an accompaniment.

SPINACH SOUP WITH PRAWNS

Spinach and prawns are a classic combination in oriental cooking, especially with the added spice of ginger. Although low in fat, prawns are said to be high in cholesterol, which does not make this an ideally healthy soup for those with high cholesterol levels. It is, on the other hand, high in calcium, especially if chard is used in preference to summer spinach.

700 g / 1½ lb prawns in their shells　　　*4–6 cloves garlic, peeled and chopped*
1.5 litres / 2½ pints water　　　　　　　*1 thimble-sized piece ginger root,*
900 g / 2 lb spinach　　　　　　　　　　　　*peeled and chopped*
sea salt

Shell the prawns and set them on one side. Cover the shells and heads with the water and simmer them, covered, for 30 minutes to make a stock. Meanwhile wash the spinach in 2 or 3 changes of water, discarding any thick stalks and ragged or slimy leaves, and cook it quite fast in its own water with a pinch of sea salt for 5–10 minutes until it has softened. Proper spinach needs little cooking; but chard or perpetual spinach, with its tougher, straighter leaves, takes longer. As soon as you hear the spinach bubbling in its own liquid, remove the lid, stir the spinach round a little and raise the heat from medium to high, taking care not to let the spinach burn. Crush the garlic and ginger together in a mortar with a little sea salt and add them to the spinach, lowering the heat again to simmering-point. Stir and leave to cook gently together for 5–10 minutes. Pour on the strained prawn stock and continue simmering for a little longer, then add the prawns and remove from the heat at once before they have time to become leathery. Liquidize and serve. A delicately spicy, fresh-tasting soup of an attractive pinkish-green.

LEEK, KIPPER AND OATFLAKE SOUP

If your household includes a traditionalist kipper-lover, he (or she) may not appreciate meeting kippers in soup. This sustaining meal in a soup-plate is worth trying at least once, however. While the two strong tastes of leeks and kippers are not usually encountered together, they are successfully married in this soup by the oats (ordinary porridge oats will do), which also help to counteract the oiliness of the kippers.

4 large leeks	1–2 teaspoons sea salt
3 tablespoons olive oil	2 kippers
2 carrots, peeled and chopped	175 g/6 oz oatflakes
1.75 litres/3 pints water	

Wash the leeks, slitting them along either side from just above the base to the crown to release trapped pockets of grit and removing the base and coarsest green parts of each. Chop them into 2.5 cm/1 in long sections, halving these crossways if the leeks are very fat, and soften them in 3 table-spoons of olive oil in a heavy, covered pan. Add the carrots and continue softening for another 10–15 minutes, stirring every now and again and making sure that the heat is kept low. Cover with the water and sea salt, bring to the boil and simmer for 15–20 minutes. Meanwhile grill the kippers for 5 minutes on each side and carefully flake off the meat, discarding the skin and all the bones. Double-check for any bones which you may have missed the first time. Add the kipper meat and oats to the soup, leave it standing for a moment until they have heated through, then liquidize. If the result seems too much like porridge, dilute with more water and reheat; but the soup should be thick, and is best treated as a main dish.

SALMON-HEAD SOUP WITH PARSLEY

While lacking the rich, curdy flakes of pink flesh which you find in steaks of the best wild salmon, farmed salmon-heads are a very acceptable alternative for soup. Like the brown meat of poultry, their flesh is distinctive and characterful in taste and makes an excellent mayonnaise. Farmed salmon-steaks can taste dull when compared with the equivalents from wild salmon; but where heads are concerned there is little point in making comparisons. Half a dozen heads, costing roughly the same at the fishmonger's as 450g/1 lb of prawns in the shell, can provide enough stock for a fish-and-vegetable soup and enough meat for six good helpings of salmon mayonnaise. Combining the two, you can have a light, frothy, salmon soup with enough meat over for some small savoury accompaniment, perhaps the cook's own lunch the following day.

6 salmon-heads

3–3.5 litres/5–6 pints water

sea salt

bayleaf (optional)

4 eggs

4 tablespoons chopped parsley

juice of 1 lemon

freshly ground black pepper

The day before serving this soup, buy the salmon-heads and cook them. To accommodate six heads you will need either a very large saucepan or 2 separate ones, in which you should simmer the heads in just-boiling, lightly salted water (to cover) for 20 minutes. Remove the heads with a slotted spoon, strip off the flesh from the bones and leave it in a covered bowl in the refrigerator. Return the bones to the saucepan, bring back the contents to the boil and simmer, with a pinch of salt and a bayleaf if you have one, for another 40 minutes. Strain the stock, discard the bones and refrigerate the cooled stock overnight. By the next day it should be jellied with a slight surface layer of fat which can be skimmed off.

Tip the skimmed stock, of which there should be 2.5–3 litres/4–5 pints, into a fairly large saucepan, boil it up and reduce it by boiling steadily, uncovered, for 10–15 minutes until it measures about 1.75 litres/3 pints. Meanwhile mix the beaten eggs, the chopped parsley and the lemon juice together and liquidize them with about half the salmon meat. Keep the rest for another occasion or serve it separately as a mayonnaise after the soup. Season the boiling stock with freshly ground black pepper and pour a good cupful of it into the liquidized mixture, swirling it well round. Once it has thickened through contact with the eggs, add a further cupful, then gradually stir in the rest of the stock until you have a pale, frothy soup, well thickened and flecked with green and pink. Pour this back into the saucepan and heat it gently for a minute or two, allowing the finely shredded salmon meat to heat through but taking care that the eggs do not separate and scramble or curdle. Pour into bowls and serve hot with plenty of brown bread and butter.

SAMPHIRE AND SCALLOPS

If samphire is in season, as it is in late summer and early autumn, you might like to make an all-fish meal by accompanying Salmon-head Soup with Parsley with a light main course of samphire and scallops.

900 g/2 lb samphire
4 large cloves garlic, peeled
2 tablespoons olive oil

12 scallops
6–8 tablespoons Marsala

Strip the samphire leaves from their stalks, allowing 900 g/2 lb of samphire for 6 people, and boil them in unsalted water for 5–10 minutes until they are soft. Soften the sliced cloves of garlic for 5–10 minutes in 2 tablespoons of olive oil, then add the scallops, omitting the coral, and stir them with the garlic over a medium heat for 2–3 minutes. Add the coral, then the drained samphire, then 6–8 tablespoons of Marsala and stir together for a further minute. Serve in shells, with a helping of samphire in each and the scallops resting on top. Allow plenty of wholemeal bread to absorb the rich sauce.

SALMON-HEAD, PRAWN AND SORREL SOUP

A fresh, green soup with a pleasantly astringent, fishy taste. If you can grow enough sorrel to harvest a colanderful or two at a time, it is worth doing so for its smoothness in soup and its sharp, clean taste whether cooked or raw in salad.

6 salmon-heads

3–3.5 litres / 5–6 pints water

700 g / 1½ lb prawns in their shells

1 teaspoon sea salt

freshly ground black pepper

450 g / 1 lb sorrel leaves, washed

4 eggs

juice of 3 lemons

Rinse the salmon-heads, cover them with water in one or two large saucepans, bring to the boil and simmer for 20 minutes. Remove the salmon-heads, strip them of their meat and return the bones to the stock to simmer for another 40 minutes. Keep the meat for a mayonnaise or another dish. Shell the prawns, put them on one side to serve separately with the soup and add the prawn shells to the stock to enrich it. Season with 1 teaspoon of sea salt and some freshly ground black pepper.

When the stock is ready, strain it into another saucepan and boil it up again to reduce it to about 1.75 litres/3 pints. Add the well-washed sorrel and continue simmering for a minute or two until this has changed colour and softened. Beat the eggs in a large bowl, add the lemon juice to them and pour in a cupful of the soup, swirling it well round until the mixture has thickened. Continue the process until the soup has been entirely mixed with the beaten eggs and lemon juice. Return the mixture to the saucepan and heat gently, stirring, until it is well thickened. Liquidize and serve, with a separate dish of prawns and lemon juice and with brown bread and butter.

NOTE

Another version of this frothy, green soup can be made using summer spinach instead of sorrel, with 1 teaspoon of freshly grated nutmeg. Do not use chard, as this will be too rough.

SALMON-HEAD AND SPINACH SOUP

A good, thin, smooth spinach soup to make the day after buying salmon for a mayonnaise.

6 salmon-heads
3–3.5 litres/5–6 pints water
sea salt
bayleaf (optional)
freshly ground black pepper

1.35 kg/3 lb spinach (not chard)
6–8 large cloves garlic
25 g/1 oz butter
juice of 2 lemons

Make stock the previous day, following the instructions given in the recipe for Salmon-head Soup with Parsley (p. 150), reduce it to about 1.75 litres/3 pints and refrigerate it overnight. When making the soup, remove the stock from the refrigerator and skim off the surface layer of fat. Wash the spinach well, pack it into a large, lidded saucepan and cook it fast for 5 minutes in the water from the leaves, sprinkling on a pinch of sea salt and stirring this well in. When the spinach has subsided, press it down and pour off most of the liquid. Peel and slice the garlic cloves and add these to the spinach with the butter. Stir round together, then cook gently for a few minutes with the lid on until the garlic has transferred its flavour to the spinach. Pour on the stock, bring it to the boil, simmer it for 5–10 minutes, then cool it slightly and liquidize. Before serving, season with salt, freshly ground black pepper and lemon juice.

SARDINE AND TOMATO SOUP

A cheerful, stimulating soup. Sardines are among the most vigorously flavoured North Atlantic fish, and therefore one of the most reliable in soup. If the procedure seems fiddly, the result can be worthwhile.

900 g/2 lb fresh, whole sardines
1.75 litres/3 pints water
2 potatoes, scrubbed and halved
sea salt
6 black peppercorns
2 onions, peeled and chopped
2 tablespoons olive oil

6–8 cloves garlic, peeled and chopped
2 400 g/14 oz tins chopped tomatoes
fresh thyme or marjoram
freshly ground black pepper
pinch of sugar (optional)
2 glasses good red or white wine
2 tablespoons extra virgin olive oil

Wash and de-scale the sardines. A surprising number of large, transparent scales, like layers of clear plastic sheeting, will accumulate at the bottom of the washing water. Behead and gut the sardines, or ask your fishmonger to do so, then fillet each one by slitting it along the line of the backbone with the point of a sharp knife and removing as much flesh as you can with a sideways sweep of the blade. Put the fillets on one side to keep cool, then cover the heads and bones with the water in a saucepan, add the potatoes, 1 teaspoon of sea salt and half a dozen black peppercorns, bring to the boil and simmer for 15–20 minutes. Meanwhile make a tomato sauce by softening the peeled and chopped onions in 2 tablespoons of olive oil, then adding the tomatoes, the chopped garlic cloves and the herbs and simmering uncovered until it is thick. Season with salt, pepper and a little sugar if needed. Remove the potatoes from the stock, add them with the uncooked sardine fillets to the tomato sauce, strain the stock over them, add the wine, bring the soup to the boil and simmer it for another 5–10 minutes. Liquidize, or put through a *moulin-légumes* if you are nervous of bones. Stir in an extra 2 tablespoons of the best olive oil and reheat before serving.

WHITE FISH AND TOMATO SOUP WITH BULGUR WHEAT

Very much a meal in itself, this soup might almost be classified as a fish stew. It is delicious, largely thanks to the bulgur wheat, whose chewy texture and grainy flavour perfectly balance the fish and the acidity of the tomatoes. Produced chiefly in Turkey and Armenia, this nourishing filler appears in Armenian lentil, tomato and meat soups, and caught on in the 1960s Californian-inspired health-food craze as an ingredient of many vegetarian soups and stews. Taste and food-value apart, it has a fluffy lightness which makes it especially attractive when combined with other light, delicate foods such as fish.

225 g/8 oz prawns in their shells
850 ml–1.2 litres/1½–2 pints water
700 g/1½ lb tomatoes
2 tablespoons olive oil
1 teaspoon sugar
sea salt

8 green peppercorns, crushed
4 cloves garlic, peeled and chopped
450 g/1 lb flaky white fish (e.g.
  whiting, cod, hoki)
110 g/4 oz bulgur wheat

Shell the prawns and make stock from the shells with the water. Skin the tomatoes after immersing them in a bowlful of near-boiling water and place them in a large, open pan over a gentle heat. Stir in 1 tablespoon of oil, 1 teaspoon of sugar, a pinch of sea salt, the crushed green peppercorns and the garlic. Break up the tomatoes as much as you can, since this soup is best left unliquidized. Put the fish to bake in a moderately hot oven, 190–200°C, 375–400°F, gas mark 5–6, for about 20 minutes, brushing it generously with olive oil beforehand and pouring on any spare juice which has been given off by the tomatoes. When the fish is just cooked, flake the flesh into the tomato sauce and discard the skin and bones. Toast the bulgur for 10 minutes in a moderately hot oven, 200°C, 400°F, gas mark 6, then stir it into the tomato mixture and strain on the prawn-shell stock. Season with 1 teaspoon of sea salt, bring to the boil, cover and simmer for 15 minutes, by which time the bulgur will have expanded to thicken the soup. Serve in bowls with a few prawns arranged on the surface of each, and with rye bread and butter.

BREAD

The American poet Amy Clampitt, describing a literary pilgrimage on foot in the hills behind Porlock or Lynton, expresses her impatience on being told that a nearby cottage is the home of a Californian lady potter:

> . . . You have
> just now not the least wish to think of
> pots, or anything that might be craf-
> ted in a day and given to a kiln to harden –
> that oven smelling of no substance so in-
> dispensable as home-made bread . . .*

Once you have begun to make your own bread, it can be almost impossible to imagine a life from which this element is permanently missing. The objections raised by friends – the need to buy several pounds of flour a week, the obligation to stand in one place kneading for ten minutes at a time, the way the dough has of transferring itself to various surfaces around you – are all overridden by the sweet-smelling, golden-brown presence of your own bread. Unlike the bought kind, which is too often a dull accessory to food, a prison for sandwich-fillings or a vehicle for large quantities of butter and other spreads, home-made bread demands to be eaten for itself regardless of what is put on it. Its importance in relation to soup is self-evident; for good bread, on its own, can complement soup in such a way as to make a fully satisfying light meal. The implications for health are also important, since bread, once condemned as a stodgy mass of supposedly fattening carbohydrates, has now begun to regain its former dignity as an essential, health-giving food. Wholemeal flour, from which much home-baked bread is once again made, contains protein (11–12 per cent of all nutritional values), B vitamins and fibre, all of which are now recognized as dietary necessities. With your own choice of oil, salt and flour, in the combinations and quantities which suit you best, home-made bread can become a highly individual part of your life, while the need to

* 'The Sacred Hearth Fire', in *What the Light Was Like*, Faber, 1986.

bake it every few days can be met as automatically as the need to shop, do ordinary cooking or eat out in restaurants.

There are, inevitably, bread-making disasters which sometimes persuade the inexperienced that the whole business of home bread-making is beyond them. Either the dough is too liquid and sticks to their hands, or it is too dry and falls apart, or they let it rise for too long before putting it in the oven so that it collapses and fails to rise properly again. All of these can be overcome in time by that quality of 'feel' which teaches one that not all flours are alike, and that approximation is often more successful than precise adherence to the given quantities in a recipe. Similarly, it is best not to leave the detailed choice of ingredients to a recipe on (say) a flour packet, unless you are persuaded that you really want to use nothing but Brand X wholemeal, Brand Y malted grain brown flour with added wheatgerm, or Brand Z strong white.

What are the differences between flours? Most people know that wholemeal contains 100 per cent of the wheat, including the oily germ and the bran, large amounts of which are excluded from white flour. Wholemeal bread-making flour, however, is stronger, and incidentally much harder to find in shops, than wholemeal cake and pastry flour, which makes a feeble, close-grained kind of bread. 'Brown' flour, sometimes containing malted grains and referred to as granary, is supposed to include 85 per cent of the wheat. Some, however, is paler in appearance than other kinds. White flour, enriched with vitamins by the millers, may appear on paper actually to be nutritionally superior to wholemeal or brown. It goes staler faster in bread, however, since it lacks the natural oils which both enrich wholemeal flour and shorten its shelf-life by encouraging it to go rancid if left unused. Lacking bran, it is also much less laxative than wholemeal flour. Bitter medical controversies have raged around the importance of bran in averting gastro-intestinal disease, while most English people continue to consume their tinned soup with white, sliced bread and to throw their crusts out to the birds, the more fastidious of which may be seen to reject them.

Apart from French bread, which few of us mind buying twice a day

when on holiday in France, we generally expect our bread to have a keeping quality, demanding the use of some kind of oil or shortening.
Sunflower oil gives a good, rich mix without the saturated fattiness of the
lard which recipes on bread-flour packets sometimes recommend one to
use. Olive oil can be good, but gives the bread a strong taste which not
everybody likes in combination with jam or honey. The quantity of oil or
shortening recommended in recipes is often far too little either to enrich
the taste or to ensure that the bread will keep longer than a couple of
days. In *focaccia*, for example, the wonderful Italian olive-oil bread which
actually tastes of oil, the proportions are 150 ml/5 fl oz of oil (or about
8 tablespoons) to 900g/2 lb of flour. (I quote from Claudia Roden, *The
Food of Italy*, 1989.) A standard recipe for bread on a flour-packet specifies
25 g/1 oz of cooking fat to 1.5 kg/3.3 lb of flour. It is, of course, in the
interests of commercial bakers to make bread which does not keep too
well; but there is no need for this kind of parsimony to be carried on in the
home, especially if the oil gives the bread a positively enjoyable taste
instead of a merely neutral one. Nor is there any point in freezing bread
unless you live alone and bake it only once a week or once a fortnight.
Bread made with an adequate amount of oil, rather less than in *focaccia* but
more than the amount usually recommended on flour packets, keeps fresh
for three, four or five days and will not harden if stored cut-side down-
wards. To preserve a good crust it should be kept somewhere where it has
access to air, either simply out in the kitchen or in a porous earthenware
crock or in a normal, modern bread bin kept propped slightly open.

Salt is important in bread but should never be as obtrusive as the oil.
I now find most bought bread and most supermarket bakery goods over-
salted, as are many commercial products including tinned and packeted
soups. As in soup, I use only Maldon sea salt for bread, since this does not
produce that burning taste on the tongue which can result from using
chemical salt or finely ground 'Mediterranean' sea salt.

Combinations of different flours often result in more interesting kinds
of bread than single flours, whether wholemeal, malted grain or white.
Wholemeal purists may argue that only their kind is acceptable, while

elderly people with delicate digestions, children and others may refuse to touch anything but white. Between these extremes, however, lies a range of possibilities with room for a certain amount of adaptation and experimentation. Finding wholemeal dull, unless made with mountain spring water and the freshest of flour, I prefer a mixture of wholemeal and brown malted grain flour in the proportions either of one to one or of two-fifths wholemeal (half a 1.5 kg/3.3 lb packet) to three-fifths malted grain (a whole 2.2 lb packet). I give this recipe here, since it is unlikely to be found in any other published source.

WHOLEMEAL/GRANARY BREAD

MAKES 3 SMALL LOAVES AND 6 ROLLS

730 g/1.65 lb strong wholemeal flour
925 g/2.2 lb brown malted grain flour
1 tablespoon sea salt

2 6 g sachets easy-bake dried yeast
75 ml/3 fl oz or more sunflower oil
1 litre/1¾ pints warm water, cooled to blood heat

Empty the flour into a large bowl and stir in the salt and easy-bake yeast. Make a well in the centre and pour in the oil. After the first few times you will probably do this by eye without measuring it. Rub the oil into the flour, then repeat the well and fill it this time with the warm water, which should come level with the top of the circular rampart of flour. Work the flour into the water with one hand, drawing the walls together in the centre and bringing up more dry flour from below to work it in. When you have a cohesive ball of dough, or something approaching one, tip it out on to a floured board and surround it with any remaining loose flour from the bowl. Mix in a little more water with this if necessary and add it to the main ball of dough. Now knead the ball for 10 minutes, giving it a quarter-turn clockwise with your right hand while pushing the opposite edge upwards and into the centre with your left. (Left-handed people may adopt the opposite procedure.) When the dough begins to sigh with a faint popping of air bubbles on the surface it is ready to rise. Return it to the bowl, cover it with a cloth and leave it in a warm place for 1–2 hours (not longer, or it will rise and collapse again and the yeast will begin to taste bitter). Punch down the dough, which should have doubled in bulk, and divide it into loaves and rolls. Unless you have an Aga or Rayburn in which the oven is already hot, do not bother with a second rising outside the oven (if you need one, this should take only 20–30 minutes), but turn on the oven and allow the bread to rise a second time as it warms. Bake in all for 40–45 minutes including the warming-up period, setting the oven at 220°C, 425°F, gas mark 7 and removing any rolls after 30–35 minutes.

Unlike buns made of soft dough with egg, sugar, butter, yeast and milk, which will cook in a hot oven in 15 minutes, wholemeal and wholemeal/granary rolls can be treated almost indistinguishably from loaves of bread. Unless they are tiny, rolls made of a heavyish dough need almost as long as small loaves to cook through. It is a good idea to turn them upside-down 5 minutes or so before removing them from the oven to allow them to brown evenly, and to turn the loaves or decant them from their tins and return them directly to the oven shelves when you remove the rolls.

HERB BREAD

MAKES 2 LARGE OR 4 SMALL LOAVES

Good with soup, especially at parties. Make following the instructions given in the recipe for Wholemeal/Granary Bread, or with one-third strong white or plain brown bread flour to two-thirds wholemeal flour.

With a generous amount of oil, this will produce bread of a nicely cake-like consistency. Towards the end of the kneading process, or after the first rising, work in a mixture of chopped fresh thyme, sage, marjoram and parsley (6 tablespoons in total) and knead gently until the herbs begin to pierce the surface from within.

FOCACCIA

The nicest kind of white bread, rich with olive oil, which gives it a keeping quality of several days. It is unlikely, however, that you will be able to resist it that long, since there is something peculiarly appetizing about its flat golden crust and the conventual purity of its close-textured crumb.

The essential characteristics of this bread are its flatness, which is achieved by rolling it out into a compact shape before baking, and its lavish proportion of olive oil to flour. The flattening procedure affects the eventual texture of the bread, concentrating the distribution and taste of the olive oil. Otherwise it is as easy to make as ordinary bread, and need not be made with white if you prefer a brown or wholemeal/granary mixture.

MAKES 2–3 LOAVES

900 g/2 lb strong white flour	150 ml/5 fl oz olive oil
½ tablespoon sea salt	570 ml/1 pint warm water, cooled to
1 6 g sachet easy-bake dried yeast	blood heat

Make the bread following the instructions given in the recipe for Wholemeal/Granary Bread (p. 164) and leave to rise for 1 hour in the bowl. Once it has risen, divide it into 2 or 3 portions and roll or flatten each of these into a disc measuring 1–3 cm/½–1½ in thick. Claudia Roden (*The Food of Italy*, 1989), from whom I have taken my quantities, specifies a thickness of 1 cm/½ in, but a very good bread can still result from a slightly less well-flattened dough, resembling more closely the *pane all'olio di uliva* of Venice than the traditional, flat *focaccia* of the quality bakeries in Mantua and other nearby cities. Fit each loaf into a round, low-sided tin and brush more olive oil generously over the top of each. Failing enough 20 to 25.5 cm/8 to 10 inch sandwich tins, you may bake two loaves side by side in a large meat tin. Allow the loaves to rise in the oven as it warms to 200°C, 400°F, gas mark 6, and leave them in altogether for 30–35 minutes until they are golden brown and sound hollow when tapped underneath. If the underside is pale, cook reversed for the last 5 minutes.

NOTE

As hearth-bread, cooked on a shovel among the ashes, this kind of bread traditionally had extra flavourings to make it a satisfying snack or small, savoury meal. Geraldene Holt (*French Country Kitchen*, 1987) describes the South French *fougasse*, an obvious cousin of *focaccia*, enriched with fried snippets of fat pork-skin. Claudia Roden describes an alternative, herb-flavoured dough, with chopped black olives mixed into it and sprinkled, with olive oil, on the top. This version is particularly good with a coarser, wholemeal/granary or brown *focaccia*, and goes well with any soup containing tomatoes or garlic.

RYE MILK-BREAD

Rye breads vary enormously from country to country, depending on the heaviness of the flour and on the extent to which it is mixed with other

ingredients. There is the deep chocolate-coloured rye bread usually associated with Germany; the lighter French *pain de seigle*, which I always buy
when in France in preference to conventional 'French' bread; the
Scandinavian rye breads, different again; and the Jewish rye bread with
caraway seeds, familiar enough in North London and on the Upper West
Side in New York.

Many of the rye breads sold in bakers' shops in western Europe and the
United States must in fact contain a high proportion of white flour, since
unadulterated rye flour, of the kind which I buy at Neal's Yard in Oxford
and London, is too grittily coarse to make anything but the heaviest,
greyest kind of bread when used on its own. Rye bread dough has a
spongier texture than wholemeal or white dough, and the bread itself is
close-textured once it has been baked. The advantage of true rye bread,
baked with freshly milled flour, is in its nutty, wholesome taste, often
emphasized by the addition of clean-tasting caraway seeds. Some people
like to counteract the mildly sour taste of rye flour by mixing the dough
with black treacle. I prefer to enhance the bread's keeping quality by giving
it a cake-like texture with a crisp, crumbly outside crust. The use of milk
and of a high proportion of oil in the dough increases the close texture of
this kind of rye bread, but also sweetens it and makes it tempting to eat
simply on its own or lightly buttered.

MAKES 1 LOAF

---

350 g/12 oz 100 per cent rye flour	*1 6 g sachet easy-bake dried yeast*
350 g/12 oz strong white bread flour	*2 teaspoons caraway seeds (optional)*
50 g/2 oz oats	*3 tablespoons sunflower oil*
½ tablespoon sea salt	*425 ml/¾ pint milk*

To make the bread, combine the rye flour, white flour, oats, salt and
yeast in a mixing-bowl. Add the caraway seeds if you are using them
and then rub in the oil. Gently warm the milk, pour it into a well in the
centre of the other ingredients and work all together until you have

formed a consistent dough. Rye flour is stickier and less tractable than wheat flour, so you may need to hold some liquid in reserve rather than adding the whole lot at once, or keep extra flour or oats to scatter on the board while kneading. If the dough falls apart into several pieces which will not cohere without forming cracks between them then it needs more liquid. Once you have a solid ball of dough, knead it for 10 minutes, return it to the bowl, cover it and allow it to rise in a warm place for 1½–2 hours. Divide the risen dough into 2 loaves, brush their outer surfaces with a mixture of oil and milk for a crisp finish, put them in the oven and set the heat to 230–240°C, 450–475°F, gas mark 8–9. Bake for 40–45 minutes until the loaves are browned and sound hollow when tapped.

Rye/Granary Bread

A nice variation on wholemeal/granary bread, in which the wholesome, clean taste of rye is perceptible but its heavy-bodiedness is balanced by the combination of white and brown flours. The use of malted grain flour makes it unnecessary to add caraway seeds for piquancy.

MAKES 2–3 LOAVES

800 g/1¾ lb brown malted grain flour (e.g. Allinson's 'Harvester')
350 g/12 oz 100 per cent rye flour
350 g/12 oz strong white flour
1 tablespoon sea salt

2 6 g sachets easy-bake dried yeast
4 tablespoons sunflower oil
1–1.2 litres/1¾–2 pints lukewarm water

Mix the flours together in a large bowl, stir in the salt and yeast and rub in the oil. Heat the water to lukewarm and pour most of it into a well in the centre of the flour, keeping back at least 150 ml/¼ pint in case it should be needed to moisten the ball of dough. (Rye flour, lacking the glutinous cohesiveness of wheat flour, can need extra moisture halfway through the kneading process to encourage the dough to keep together in one piece.) Knead for 10 minutes, cover, and leave to stand for about 1½ hours, then divide into 2–3 loaves and bake at 220°C, 425°F, gas mark 7, for the usual 35–40 minutes. Unlike Rye Milk-bread, which has a slightly heavy, scofa-like consistency, this mixture makes delicious, light yet nourishing breakfast rolls.

WHOLEMEAL/WHITE BREAD

I have become very fond of this golden-brown bread, which has a lovely, sweet fragrance when newly baked, keeps well, and is especially suitable for breakfast rolls to eat warm with honey. The inclusion of white flour gives the dough an extra pliancy and a tendency to spread sideways, making the rolls luxuriously large and both crusty and soft.

MAKES 3 SMALL LOAVES AND 6 ROLLS

1.1 kg/2¼ lb strong wholemeal flour	*2 6 g sachets easy-bake dried yeast*
550 g/1¼ lb strong white flour	*6 tablespoons sunflower oil*
1 rounded tablespoon sea salt	*1 litre/1¾ pints lukewarm water*

Follow the instructions for Wholemeal/Granary Bread (p. 164), adapting the relative proportions of wholemeal and white flour to your own taste but making sure that the two flours are thoroughly blended together before you add the liquid and begin to knead the dough. I would on occasion use less white flour in proportion to wholemeal than the amount which I have given here, and in principle prefer to keep the amount of white used nearer to one-third than to half of the total. The function of the white flour is to give the dough elasticity and lightness, while the wholemeal gives the bread its nutty taste, its soft, brown colour and its nourishing and keeping qualities.

TOMATO AND OLIVE BREAD

If the ingredients for this recipe sound familiarly like those for pizza, the end product is quite different: crusty, rounded loaves with the savoury filling dispersed throughout the dough, making a perfect tearing-bread for lunchtime to eat with soup, cheese or scrambled eggs. This bread is at its best when newly baked and still warm, but also keeps well and can be enjoyed cold for several days after baking. The combination of brown, white and wholemeal flours gives a springy, light-brown bread which is predominantly wholemeal in character but pliable enough to contain the moist, savoury filling while remaining airy within and crisp on the outside surface.

MAKES 2 SMALL LOAVES

350 g/12 oz strong wholemeal flour	*6 fresh tomatoes, or a combination of*
110 g/4 oz strong brown flour	*fresh and sun-dried tomatoes*
110 g/4 oz strong white flour	*1 large clove garlic, peeled*
½ rounded tablespoon sea salt	*sea salt*
1 6 g sachet easy-bake dried yeast	*freshly ground black pepper*
4 tablespoons olive oil	*10 black olives, stoned*
350 ml/⅔ pint lukewarm water	*1 heaped teaspoon tomato purée*

Mix the flours together in a bowl, add the salt and the yeast, make a well in the centre and pour in 3 tablespoons of the olive oil, reserving the final tablespoon for the tomatoes. Continue making the bread as in the instructions for Wholemeal/Granary Bread (p. 164), using just enough water to produce a stiffish dough. After kneading, leave the dough to rise in a warm place while you prepare the tomato and olive filling.

Warm the final tablespoon of olive oil in a small, heavy-bottomed pan and add the skinned and quartered tomatoes, the roughly chopped sun-dried tomatoes (if you can get these, they go well in roughly equal proportions to the fresh kind), the chopped and crushed clove of garlic and a little sea salt and freshly ground black pepper. Cook gently together for 5–10 minutes while you stone the olives (which will taste much more succulent if they have not been mechanically pre-stoned), then stir in the halved, stoneless olives and the tomato purée. Mix well together until the purée, oil and garlic are well amalgamated, but do not try to reduce the tomatoes to a formless pulp. Turn off the heat and leave to cool to just below blood heat.

When the dough has risen, divide it in half, flatten out each half into a rough saucer-shape and place half the tomato and olive mixture on each. Enclose the filling in the dough (which will become quite slippery on contact with it) and form each loaf into a round shape, making sure that the filling does not pierce the surface. Place the loaves on greased tins and cut a deep cross-shape on the top of each loaf to form 4 small peaks. Bake for 30–35 minutes in a hot oven, 220°C, 425°F, gas mark 7.

SESAME ROLLED BREAD

This nourishing bread contains a generous helping of sesame seeds, not simply sprinkled on top as on Greek bread but rolled inside it in a crunchy, spiral layer somewhat like the filling of a Swiss roll. It goes well with soft cheese, honey or butter and is equally good eaten plain and newly made with soup, when it gives an extra lift to the meal with its nutty freshness and high protein content. Sesame seeds are also among the protective foods recommended by nutritionists to diminish the likelihood of coronary heart disease; and this is one of the most practicable ways of eating them, far easier than munching through them in gritty muesli form or directly and untidily from the packet.

MAKES 1 LARGE OR 2 SMALL LOAVES

450 g / 1 lb strong wholemeal flour
225 g / 8 oz strong white flour
½ rounded tablespoon sea salt
1 6 g sachet easy-bake dried yeast
2 tablespoons sunflower oil

425 ml / ¾ pint lukewarm water
25–40 g / 1–1½ oz sesame seeds
1 beaten egg
15 g / ½ oz melted butter

Using all but the last three ingredients, make the bread dough following the instructions for Wholemeal/Granary Bread. Leave the dough to rise for about 1 hour in a warm place, then flatten it on a board, divide it in half if you wish to make 2 small and relatively manageable loaves and roll each of these out to 1 cm/½ in thickness. Sprinkle a generous layer of sesame seeds to cover the entire rolled-out surface of the dough and press them down firmly with the flat of one hand. Ladle on alternate spoonfuls of beaten egg and melted butter and spread these out over the layer of sesame seeds using the underside of the spoon. (If not anchored with this mixture, the sesame seeds will simply fall out once the bread is cooked.) Roll up each loaf into a Swiss roll shape, tuck in the ends, glaze the surface with any remaining egg and bake on a flat, greased tin in a hot oven, 220°C, 425°F, gas mark 7, for 35 minutes. Eat within 2 days.

OAT BREAD

In the hilly, oat-growing areas of northern Britain, oats used to be the food of necessity: not only in the form of porridge, but in flat, unleavened oat-cakes baked slowly on a griddle and hung up while still soft to dry out. In times of great agricultural distress, in the early nineteenth century, a few oats would make a thin, faintly nourishing gruel which served as a substi-tute for both meat and bread. Oats have never ground easily into flour (except in electric blenders, which reduce them to a stiffish kind of flour, perfectly acceptable in small quantities to use in emergencies, for example in making a white sauce); so we have no native tradition of leavened oat bread, as the central European countries have of rye bread or the southern French of bread made from chestnut flour. Modern oatflakes, on the other hand, make a delicious addition to bread dough, giving it a slightly stiff texture, a good, crisp crust and a fresh, nutty flavour. Reheated breakfast rolls made with this dough are particularly interesting and good.

MAKES 2 SMALL LOAVES AND 6–8 ROLLS

800 g / 1¾ lb strong wholemeal flour
400 g / 14 oz strong white flour
275 g / 10 oz oatflakes
1 tablespoon sea salt

2 6 g sachets easy-bake dried yeast
5 tablespoons sunflower oil
850 ml / 1½ pints lukewarm water

Make the bread dough, following the instructions for Wholemeal/Granary Bread (p. 164). Keep back 50 g/2 oz of the oats from the mixture and place them on the board before kneading the dough, to be absorbed while kneading. Add the water carefully and be prepared to use more if the dough falls apart or proves too stiff and crumbly to stick together. Leave to rise for about 1 hour, then shape into loaves and rolls. The slight stiffness of the dough makes it easier to form into small, compact rolls than any other kind. Bake for 40–45 minutes at 220°C, 425°F, gas mark 7 (including warming-up period) or 30–35 minutes in a preheated oven. Turn over rolls after 20–30 minutes and remove 10 minutes before the loaves.

CORNBREAD WITH CHEESE AND SAGE

Comforting, sweet, rough-textured cornmeal has always been part of the bedrock of ordinary American life. In the early nineteenth century, American patriots and adherents to the simple life, such as Thoreau, defended its merits against those of scarce, expensive wheat flour, which seemed yet another unnecessary fashion imported from the former hated colonial power, England. William Cobbett, who had lived in America not long after the Revolution, later tried unsuccessfully to convert his fellow Englishmen to growing and eating maize; but 'Cobbett's corn', as he grandiosely called it, failed to catch on. Even now, however, corn muffins are a favourite item at breakfast in the United States, as they were two hundred years ago; and cornbread of various kinds is still popular, especially in the Midwest and the South.

This rough, golden bread, with its light, scone-like texture and crumbly outside crust, is a good accompaniment to tomato soup and a sustaining lunchtime filler. The inclusion of cheese counteracts the tendency to dryness in cornbread as well as making this bread virtually a meal in itself. Fresh sage gives a good, strong, sharp taste; but for a different, celery-like flavour try substituting lovage (best in May when the plant is newly in leaf) if you either grow it yourself or have a friend from whom you can beg some.

MAKES EITHER 1 LARGE LOAF OR 2 SMALL LOAVES

225 g/8 oz cornmeal
225 g/8 oz strong white flour
1 rounded teaspoon sea salt
1 6 g sachet easy-bake dried yeast
2 tablespoons sunflower oil

110 g/4 oz grated Cheddar cheese
275 ml/½ pint lukewam water
25–50 g/1–2 oz oatflakes (optional)
1–2 tablespoons chopped fresh sage
  leaves

Put the cornmeal, flour, salt, yeast, oil and grated cheese together in a bowl. Rub in the oil and cheese until they are well mixed with the cornmeal and flour, then add the water gradually and work it into the dry ingredients until you have a consistent ball. If the mixture seems too sticky to knead, add the oatflakes or more flour. Knead, leave to rise for 1–2 hours, incorporate the sage leaves into the dough, then divide the dough to make 2 small loaves or leave it as 1 large one. Bake the bread for 45–50 minutes in a hot oven, 220°C, 425°F, gas mark 7, reducing the heat to 200°C, 400°F, gas mark 6 for the last 15 minutes.

BIBLIOGRAPHY

Acton, Eliza, *Modern Cookery for Private Families* (1845). Abridged as *The Best of Eliza Acton*, selected and edited by Elizabeth Ray with an introduction by Elizabeth David (Longman, 1968).

Burnett, John, *Plenty & Want: A Social History of Food in England from 1815 to the Present Day* (Routledge, 3rd edition, 1989).

Castelvetro, Giacomo, *The Fruit, Herbs and Vegetables of Italy*, translated with an introduction by Gillian Riley (Viking, 1989).

Chamberlain, Lesley, *The Food and Cooking of Eastern Europe* (Penguin, 1989).

Chao, Buwei Yang, *How to Cook and Eat in Chinese* (Penguin, 1962).

Chatto, James, and Martin, W.L., *A Kitchen in Corfu*, (Weidenfeld and Nicholson, 1987).

David, Elizabeth, *Italian Food* (Penguin, revised edition, 1963).
  A Book of Mediterranean Food (Penguin, revised edition, 1965).
  French Country Cooking (Penguin, 2nd revised edition, 1966).
  French Provincial Cooking (Penguin, 2nd revised edition, 1970).
  Spices, Salt and Aromatics in the English Kitchen (Penguin, 1970).

Drummond, J.C., and Wilbraham, Anne, *The Englishman's Food: Five Centuries of English Diet*, revised and with a new chapter by D.F. Hollingsworth (Jonathan Cape, 1958).

Francatelli, Charles Elmé, *The Cook's Guide, and Housekeeper's & Butler's Assistant: a practical treatise on English and foreign cookery in all its branches* (Richard Bentley, 1861).

Gray, Patience, *Honey from a Weed* (Papermac, 1987).

Grigson, Jane, *Good Things* (Penguin, 1973).
  English Food (Penguin, 1974).

Hanbury-Tenison, Marika, *Soups and Hors d'Oeuvres* (Penguin, 1969).
  Cooking with Vegetables (Jonathan Cape, 1980).

Hartley, Dorothy, *Food in England* (Macdonald, 1954).

Holt, Geraldene, *French Country Kitchen* (Penguin, 1987).

Howe, Robin, *Soups* (International Wine and Food Society, 1967).

Innes, Jocasta, *The Pauper's Cookbook* (Penguin, 1971).

Roden, Claudia, *A Book of Middle Eastern Food* (Penguin, 1970).

    The Food of Italy (Arrow, 1990).

Sass, Lorna, *To the King's Taste: Richard II's Book of Feasts and Recipes* (John Murray, 1976).

Simon, André, *Guide to Good Food and Wines* (Collins, revised edition, 1963).

Soper, Musia (ed.), *Encyclopaedia of European Cooking* (Spring Books, 1962).

Walker, Caroline, and Cannon, Geoffrey, *The Food Scandal* (Century Arrow, 1986).

Woodforde, James, *Diary of a Country Parson, 1758–1802*, selected and edited by John Beresford (World's Classics, 1949).

Wright, Hannah, *Soups* (Robert Hale, 1985).

INDEX